The Divine Comedy Of Dante Alighieri, Volume 1

CONTENTS.

———◆———

CANTO X.

CANTO XI.

CANTO XII.

CANTO XIII.

CANTO XIV.

CANTO XV.

CANTO XVI.

CANTO XVII.

CANTO XVIII.

CANTO XIX.

CANTO XX.

CANTO XXXIII.

CANTO XXXIV.

INTRODUCTION.

So many versions of the *Divine Comedy* exist in English that a new one might well seem needless. But most of these translations are in verse, and the intellectual temper of our time is impatient of a transmutation in which substance is sacrificed for form's sake, and the new form is itself different from the original. The conditions of verse in different languages vary so widely as to make any versified translation of a poem but an imperfect reproduction of the archetype. It is like an imperfect mirror that renders but a partial likeness, in which essential features are blurred or distorted. Dante himself, the first modern critic, declared that "nothing harmonized by a musical bond can be transmuted from its own speech without losing all its sweetness and harmony," and every fresh attempt at translation affords a new proof of the truth of his assertion. Each language exhibits its own special genius in its poetic forms. Even when they are closely similar in rhythmical method their poetic effect is essentially different, their individuality is distinct. The hexameter of the *Iliad* is not the hexameter of the *Æneid*. And if this be the case in respect to related forms, it is even more obvious in respect to forms peculiar to one language, like the *terza rima* of the Italian, for which it is impossible to find a satisfactory equivalent in another tongue.

If, then, the attempt be vain to reproduce the form or to represent its effect in a translation, yet the substance of a poem may have such worth that it deserves to be known by readers who must read it in their own tongue or not at all. In this case the aim of the translator should be to render the substance fully, exactly, and with as close a correspondence to the tone and style of the original as is possible between prose and poetry. Of the charm, of the power of the poem such a translation can give but an inadequate suggestion; the musical bond was of its essence, and the loss of the musical bond is the loss of the beauty to which form and substance mutually contributed, and in which they were both alike harmonized and sublimated. The rhythmic life of the original is its vital spirit, and the translation losing this vital spirit is at best as the dull plaster cast to the living marble or the breathing bronze. The intellectual substance is there; and if the work be good, something of the emotional quality may be

conveyed; the imagination may mould the prose
as it moulded the verse, — but, after all, " translations are but as turn-coated things at best," as
Howell said in one of his *Familiar Letters.*

No poem in any tongue is more informed with
rhythmic life than the *Divine Comedy.* And
yet, such is its extraordinary distinction, no poem
has an intellectual and emotional substance more
independent of its metrical form. Its complex
structure, its elaborate measure and rhyme, highly
artificial as they are, are so mastered by the genius
of the poet as to become the most natural expression of the spirit by which the poem is inspired;
while at the same time the thought and sentiment
embodied in the verse is of such import, and the
narrative of such interest, that they do not lose
their worth when expressed in the prose of another
tongue; they still have power to quicken imagination, and to evoke sympathy.

In English there is an excellent prose translation of the *Inferno,* by Dr. John Carlyle, a man
well known to the reader of his brother's Correspondence. It was published forty years ago, but
it is still contemporaneous enough in style to answer every need, and had Dr. Carlyle made a version of the whole poem I should hardly have cared
to attempt a new one. In my translation of the
Inferno I am often Dr. Carlyle's debtor. His

conception of what a translation should be is very
much the same as my own. Of the *Purgatorio*
there is a prose version which has excellent qualities, by Mr. W. S. Dugdale. Another version of
great merit, of both the *Purgatorio* and *Paradiso*,
is that of Mr. A. J. Butler. It is accompanied by
a scholarly and valuable comment, and I owe much
to Mr. Butler's work. But through what seems to
me occasional excess of literal fidelity his English
is now and then somewhat crabbed. " He overacts
the office of an interpreter," I cite again from
Howell, " who doth enslave himself too strictly to
words or phrases. One may be so over-punctual in
words that he may mar the matter."

I have tried to be as literal in my translation as
was consistent with good English, and to render
Dante's own words in words as nearly correspond-
ent to them as the difference in the languages
would permit. But it is to be remembered that
the familiar uses and subtle associations which
give to words their full meaning are never abso-
lutely the same in two languages. *Love* in English not only *sounds* but *is* different from *amor*
in Latin, or *amore* in Italian. Even the most
felicitous prose translation must fail therefore at
times to afford the entire and precise meaning of
the original.

Moreover, there are difficulties in Dante's poem

for Italians, and there are difficulties in the translation for English readers. These, where it seemed
needful, I have endeavored to explain in brief foot-
notes. But I have desired to avoid distracting the
attention of the reader from the narrative, and
have mainly left the understanding of it to his
good sense and perspicacity. The clearness of
Dante's imaginative vision is so complete, and the
character of his narration of it so direct and simple, that the difficulties in understanding his intention are comparatively few.

It is a noticeable fact that in by far the greater
number of passages where a doubt in regard to
the interpretation exists, the obscurity lies in the
rhyme-word. For with all the abundant resources
of the Italian tongue in rhyme, and with all
Dante's mastery of them, the truth still is that his
triple rhyme often compelled him to exact from
words such service as they did not naturally render and as no other poet had required of them.
The compiler of the *Ottimo Comento* records, in
an often-cited passage, that "I, the writer, heard
Dante say that never a rhyme had led him to say
other than he would, but that many a time and oft
he had made words say for him what they were
not wont to express for other poets." The sentence has a double truth, for it indicates not only
Dante's incomparable power to compel words to

give out their full meaning, but also his invention of new uses for them, his employment of them in unusual significations or in forms hardly elsewhere to be found. These devices occasionally interfere with the limpid flow of his diction, but the difficulties of interpretation to which they give rise serve rather to mark the prevailing clearness and simplicity of his expression than seriously to impede its easy and unperplexed current. There are few sentences in the *Divina Commedia* in which a difficulty is occasioned by lack of definiteness of thought or distinctness of image.

A far deeper-lying and more pervading source of imperfect comprehension of the poem than any verbal difficulty exists in the double or triple meaning that runs through it. The narrative of the poet's spiritual journey is so vivid and consistent that it has all the reality of an account of an actual experience; but within and beneath runs a stream of allegory not less consistent and hardly less continuous than the narrative itself. To the illustration and carrying out of this interior meaning even the minutest details of external incident are made to contribute, with an appropriateness of significance, and with a freedom from forced interpretation or artificiality of construction such as no other writer of allegory has succeeded in attaining. The poem may be read with interest as a record of experience without attention to its inner meaning, but its full interest is only felt when this inner meaning is traced, and the moral significance of the incidents of the story apprehended by the alert intelligence. The allegory is the soul of the poem, but like the soul within the body it does not show itself in independent existence. It is, in scholastic phrase, the form of the body, giving to it its special individuality.

Thus in order truly to understand and rightly appreciate the poem the reader must follow its course with a double intelligence. " Taken literally," as Dante declares in his Letter to Can Grande, " the subject is the state of the soul after death, simply considered. But, allegorically taken, its subject is man, according as by his good or ill deserts he renders himself liable to the reward or punishment of Justice." It is the allegory of human life; and not of human life as an abstraction, but of the individual life; and herein, as Mr. Lowell, whose phrase I borrow, has said, " lie its profound meaning and its permanent force." [1] And herein too lie its perennial freshness of interest, and the actuality which makes it contem-

---

[1] Mr. Lowell's essay on Dante makes other writing about the poet or the poem seem ineffectual and superfluous. I must assume that it will be familiar to the readers of my version, at least to those among them who desire truly to understand the *Divine Comedy.*

poraneous with every successive generation. The increase of knowledge, the loss of belief in doctrines that were fundamental in Dante's creed, the changes in the order of society, the new thoughts of the world, have not lessened the moral import of the poem, any more than they have lessened its excellence as a work of art. Its real substance is as independent as its artistic beauty, of science, of creed, and of institutions. Human nature has not changed; the motives of action are the same, though their relative force and the desires and ideals by which they are inspired vary from generation to generation. And thus it is that the moral judgments of life framed by a great poet whose imagination penetrates to the core of things, and who, from his very nature as poet, conceives and sets forth the issues of life not in a treatise of abstract morality, but by means of sensible types and images, never lose interest, and have a perpetual contemporaneousness. They deal with the permanent and unalterable elements of the soul of man.

The scene of the poem is the spiritual world, of which we are members even while still denizens in the world of time. In the spiritual world the results of sin or perverted love, and of virtue or right love, in this life of probation, are manifest. The life to come is but the fulfilment of the life that now is. This is the truth that Dante sought to enforce. The allegory in which he cloaked it is of a character that separates the *Divine Comedy* from all other works of similar intent. In *The Pilgrim's Progress*, for example, the personages introduced are mere simulacra of men and women, the types of moral qualities or religious dispositions. They are abstractions which the genius of Bunyan fails to inform with vitality sufficient to kindle the imagination of the reader with a sense of their actual, living and breathing existence. But in the *Divine Comedy* the personages are all from real life, they are men and women with their natural passions and emotions, and they are undergoing an actual experience. The allegory consists in making their characters and their fates, what all human characters and fates really are, the types and images of spiritual law. Virgil and Beatrice, whose nature as depicted in the poem makes nearest approach to purely abstract and typical existence, are always consistently presented as living individuals, exalted indeed in wisdom and power, but with hardly less definite and concrete humanity than that of Dante himself.

The scheme of the created Universe held by the Christians of the Middle Ages was comparatively simple, and so definite that Dante, in accepting it in its main features without modification, was provided with the limited stage that was requisite for his design, and of which the general disposition was familiar to all his readers. The three spiritual realms had their local bounds marked out as clearly as those of the earth itself. Their cosmography was but an extension of the largely hypothetical geography of the time.

The Earth was the centre of the Universe, and its northern hemisphere was the abode of man. At the middle point of this hemisphere stood Jerusalem, equidistant from the Pillars of Hercules on the West, and the Ganges on the East.

Within the body of this hemisphere was Hell, shaped as a vast cone, of which the apex was the centre of the globe; and here, according to Dante, was the seat of Lucifer. The concave of Hell had been formed by his fall, when a portion of the solid earth, through fear of him, ran back to the southern uninhabited hemisphere, and formed there, directly antipodal to Jerusalem, the mountain of Purgatory which rose from the waste of waters that covered this half of the globe. Purgatory was shaped as a cone, of similar dimensions to that of Hell, and at its summit was the Terrestrial Paradise.

Immediately surrounding the atmosphere of the Earth was the sphere of elemental fire. Around this was the Heaven of the Moon, and encircling this, in order, were the Heavens of Mercury, Venus, the Sun, Mars, Jove, Saturn, the Fixed Stars, and the Crystalline or first moving Heaven. These nine concentric Heavens revolved continually around the Earth, and in proportion to their distance from it was the greater swiftness of each. Encircling all was the Empyrean, increate, incorporeal, motionless, unbounded in time or space, the proper seat of God, the home of the Angels, the abode of the Elect.

The Angelic Hierarchy consisted of nine orders, corresponding to the nine moving Heavens. Their blessedness and the swiftness of the motion with which in unending delight they circled around God were in proportion to their nearness to Him, — first the Seraphs, then the Cherubs, Thrones, Dominations, Virtues, Powers, Princes, Archangels, and Angels. Through them, under the general name of Intelligences, the Divine influence was transmitted to the Heavens, giving to them their circular motion, which was the expression of their longing to be united with the source of their creation. The Heavens in their turn streamed down upon the Earth the Divine influence thus distributed among them, in varying proportion and power, producing divers effects in the generation and corruption of material things, and in the dispositions and the lives of men.

Such was the general scheme of the Universe. The intention of God in its creation was to communicate of his own perfection to the creatures endowed with souls, that is, to men and to angels, and the proper end of every such creature was to seek its own perfection in likeness to the Divine. This end was attained through that knowledge of God of which the soul was capable, and through love which was in proportion to knowledge. Virtue depended on the free will of man ; it was the good use of' that will directed to a right object of love. Two lights were given to the soul for guidance of the will: the light of reason for natural things and for the direction of the will to moral virtue ; the light of grace for things supernatural, and for the direction of the will to spiritual virtue. Sin was the opposite of virtue, the choice by the will of false objects of love ; it involved the misuse of reason, and the absence of grace. As the end of virtue was blessedness, so the end of sin was misery.

The corner-stone of Dante's moral system was the Freedom of the Will ; in other words, the right of private judgment with the condition of accountability. This is the liberty which Dante, that is man, goes seeking in his journey through the spiritual world. This liberty is to be attained through the right use of reason, illuminated by Divine

Grace; it consists in the perfect accord of the will of man with the will of God.

With this view of the nature and end of man Dante's conception of the history of the race could not be other than that its course was providentially ordered. The fall of man had made him a just object of the vengeance of God; but the elect were to be redeemed, and for their redemption the history of the world from the beginning was directed. Not only in his dealings with the Jews, but in his dealings with the heathen was God preparing for the reconciliation of man, to be finally accomplished in his sacrifice of Himself for them. The Roman Empire was foreordained and established for this end. It was to prepare the way for the establishment of the Roman Church. It was the appointed instrument for the political government of men. Empire and Church were alike divine institutions for the guidance of man on earth.

The aim of Dante in the *Divine Comedy* was to set forth these truths in such wise as to affect the imaginations and touch the hearts of men, so that they should turn to righteousness. His conviction of these truths was no mere matter of belief; it had the ardor and certainty of faith. They had appeared to him in all their fulness as a revelation of the Divine wisdom. It was his work as poet, as poet with a divine commission, to make this revelation known. His work was a work of faith; it was sacred; to it both Heaven and Earth had set their hands.

To this work, as I have said, the definiteness and the limits of the generally accepted theory of the Universe gave the required frame. The very narrowness of this scheme made Dante's design practicable. He had had the experience of a man on earth. He had been lured by false objects of desire from the pursuit of the true good. But Divine Grace, in the form of Beatrice, who had of old on earth led him aright, now intervened and sent to his aid Virgil, who, as the type of Human Reason, should bring him safe through Hell, showing to him the eternal consequences of sin, and then should conduct him, penitent, up the height of Purgatory, till on its summit, in the Earthly Paradise, Beatrice should appear once more to him. Thence she, as the type of that knowledge through which comes the love of God, should lead him, through the Heavens up to the Empyrean, to the consummation of his course in the actual vision of God.

AIDS TO THE STUDY OF THE DIVINE COMEDY.

THE Essay by Mr. Lowell, to which I have already referred (*Dante*, Lowell's Prose Works, vol. iv.) is the best introduction to the study of the poem. It should be read and re-read.

Dante, an essay by the late Dean Church, is the work of a learned and sympathetic scholar, and is an excellent treatise on the life, times, and work of the poet.

The Notes and Illustrations that accompany Mr. Longfellow's translation of the *Divine Comedy* form an admirable body of comment on the poem.

The Rev. Dr. Edward Moore's little volume, on *The Time-References in the Divina Commedia* (London, 1887), is of great value in making the progress of Dante's journey clear, and in showing Dante's scrupulous consistency of statement. Dr. Moore's more recent work, *Contributions to the Textual Criticism of the Divina Commedia* (Cambridge, 1889), is to be warmly commended to the advanced student.

These sources of information are enough for the mere English reader. But one who desires to make himself a thorough master of the poem must turn to foreign sources of instruction: to Carl Witte's invaluable *Dante-Forschungen* (2 vols. Halle, 1869); to the comment, especially that on the *Paradiso*, which accompanies the German translation of the *Divine Comedy* by Philalethes, the late King John of Saxony; to Bartoli's life of Dante in his *Storia della Letteratura Italiana* (Firenze, 1878 and subsequent years), and to Scartazzini's *Prolegomeni della Divina Commedia* (Leipzig, 1890). The fourteenth century Comments, especially those of Boccaccio, of Buti, and of Benvenuto da Imola, are indispensable to one who would understand the poem as it was understood by Dante's immediate contemporaries and successors. It is from them and from the Chronicle of Dante's contemporary and fellow-citizen, Giovanni Villani, that our knowledge concerning many of the personages mentioned in the Poem is derived.

In respect to the theology and general doctrine of the Poem, the *Summa Theologica* of St. Thomas Aquinas is the main source from which Dante himself drew.

Of editions of the *Divina Commedia* in Italian, either that of Andreoli, or of Bianchi, or of Fraticelli, each in one volume, may be recommended to the beginner. Scartazzini's edition in three volumes is the best, in spite of some serious defects, for the deeper student.

HELL.

HELL.

CANTO I.

Dante, astray in a wood, reaches the foot of a hill which he begins to ascend; he is hindered by three beasts; he turns back and is met by Virgil, who proposes to guide him into the eternal world.

MIDWAY upon the road of our life I found myself within a dark wood, for the right way had been missed. Ah! how hard a thing it is to tell what this wild and rough and dense wood was, which in thought renews the fear! So bitter is it that death is little more. But in order to treat of the good that there I found, I will tell of the other things that I have seen there. I cannot well recount how I entered it, so full was I of slumber at that point where I abandoned the true way. But after I had arrived at the foot of a hill, where that valley ended which had pierced my heart with fear, I looked on high, and saw its shoulders clothed already with the rays of the planet[1] that leadeth men aright along every path. Then was

[1] The sun, a planet according to the Ptolemaic system.

the fear a little quieted which in the lake of my heart had lasted through the night that I passed so piteously.   And even as one who with spent breath, issued out of the sea upon the shore, turns to the perilous water and gazes, so did my soul, which still was flying, turn back to look again upon the pass which never had a living person left.

After I had rested a little my weary body I took my way again along the desert slope, so that the firm foot was always the lower.   And lo! almost at the beginning of the steep a she-leopard, light and very nimble, which was covered with a spotted coat.   And she did not move from before my face, nay, rather hindered so my road that to return I oftentimes had turned.

The time was at the beginning of the morning, and the Sun was mounting upward with those stars that were with him when Love Divine first set in motion those beautiful things;[1] so that the hour of the time and the sweet season were occasion of good hope to me concerning that wild beast with the dappled skin.   But not so that the sight which appeared to me of a lion did not give me fear.   He seemed to be coming against me, with head high and with ravening hunger, so that it seemed that

[1] According to old tradition the spring was the season of the creation.

the air was affrighted at him. And a she-wolf,[1] who with all cravings seemed laden in her meagreness, and already had made many folk to live forlorn, — she caused me so much heaviness, with the fear that came from sight of her, that I lost hope of the height. And such as he is who gaineth willingly, and the time arrives that makes him lose, who in all his thoughts weeps and is sad, — such made me the beast without repose that, coming on against me, little by little was pushing me back thither where the Sun is silent.

While I was falling back to the low place, before mine eyes appeared one who through long silence seemed hoarse. When I saw him in the great desert, "Have pity on me!" I cried to him, "whatso thou art, or shade or real man." He answered me: "Not man; man once I was, and my parents were Lombards, and Mantuans by country both. I was born *sub Julio*, though late, and I lived at Rome under the good Augustus, in the time of the false and lying gods. Poet was I, and sang of that just son of Anchises who came from Troy after proud Ilion had been burned. But thou, why returnest thou to so great annoy? Why dost thou not ascend the delectable mountain which is the source and cause of every joy?"

---

[1] These three beasts correspond to the triple division of sins into those of incontinence, of violence, and of fraud. See Canto XI.

"Art thou then that Virgil and that fount which poureth forth so large a stream of speech?" replied I to him with bashful front: " O honor and light of the other poets! may the long zeal avail me, and the great love, which have made me search thy volume! Thou art my master and my author; thou alone art he from whom I took the fair style that hath done me honor. Behold the beast because of which I turned; help me against her, famous sage, for she makes my veins and pulses tremble."
"Thee it behoves to hold another course," he replied, when he saw me weeping, "if thou wishest to escape from this savage place; for this beast, because of which thou criest out, lets not any one pass along her way, but so hinders him that she kills him; and she has a nature so malign and evil that she never sates her greedy will, and after food is hungrier than before. Many are the animals with which she wives, and there shall be more yet, till the hound [1] shall come that will make her die of grief. He shall not feed on land or goods, but wisdom and love and valor, and his birthplace shall be between Feltro and Feltro. Of that humble [2] Italy

---

[1] Of whom the hound is the symbol, and to whom Dante looked for the deliverance of Italy from the discords and misrule that made her wretched, is still matter of doubt, after centuries of controversy.

[2] Fallen, humiliated.

shall he be the salvation, for which the virgin Camilla died, and Euryalus, Turnus and Nisus of their wounds. He shall hunt her through every town till he shall have set her back in hell, there whence envy first sent her forth. Wherefore I think and deem it for thy best that thou follow me, and I will be thy guide, and will lead thee hence through the eternal place where thou shalt hear the despairing shrieks, shalt see the ancient spirits woeful who each proclaim the second death. And then thou shalt see those who are contented in the fire, because they hope to come, whenever it may be, to the blessed folk ; to whom if thou wilt thereafter ascend, there shall be a soul more worthy than I for that. With her I will leave thee at my departure ; for that Emperor who reigneth thereabove, because I was rebellious to His law, wills not that into His city any one should come through me. In all parts He governs and there He reigns : there is His city and His lofty seat. O happy he whom thereto He elects ! " And I to him, " Poet, I beseech thee by that God whom thou didst not know, in order that I may escape this ill and worse, that thou lead me thither where thou now hast said, so that I may see the gate of St. Peter, and those whom thou makest so afflicted."

Then he moved on, and I behind him kept.

CANTO II.

Dante, doubtful of his own powers, is discouraged at the outset. Virgil cheers him by telling him that he has been sent to his aid by a blessed Spirit from Heaven. Dante casts off fear, and the poets proceed.

THE day was going, and the dusky air was taking the living things that are on earth from their fatigues, and I alone was preparing to sustain the war alike of the road, and of the woe which the mind that erreth not shall retrace. O Muses, O lofty genius, now assist me! O mind that didst inscribe that which I saw, here shall thy nobility appear! I began : —

"Poet, that guidest me, consider my virtue, if it is sufficient, ere to the deep pass thou trustest me. Thou sayest that the parent of Silvius while still corruptible went to the immortal world and was there in the body. Wherefore if the Adversary of every ill was then courteous, thinking on the high effect that should proceed from him, and on the Who and the What,[1] it seemeth not unmeet to the man of understanding; for in the empyreal heaven he had been chosen for father of revered Rome and

[1] Who he was, and what should result.

of her empire; both which (to say truth indeed) were ordained for the holy place where the successor of the greater Peter hath his seat. Through this going, whereof thou givest him vaunt, he learned things which were the cause of his victory and of the papal mantle. Afterward the Chosen Vessel went thither to bring thence comfort to that faith which is the beginning of the way of salvation. But I, why go I thither? or who concedes it? I am not Aeneas, I am not Paul; me worthy of this, neither I nor others think; wherefore if I give myself up to go, I fear lest the going may be mad. Thou art wise, thou understandest better than I speak."

And as is he who unwills what he willed, and because of new thoughts changes his design, so that he quite withdraws from beginning, such I became on that dark hillside: wherefore in my thought I abandoned the enterprise which had been so hasty in the beginning.

"If I have rightly understood thy speech," replied that shade of the magnanimous one, "thy soul is hurt by cowardice, which oftentimes encumbereth a man so that it turns him back from honorable enterprise, as false seeing does a beast when it is startled. In order that thou loose thee from this fear I will tell thee wherefore I have come, and what I heard at the first moment that I grieved for thee. I was among those who are suspended,[1] and a Lady called me, so blessed and beautiful that I besought her to command. Her eyes were more lucent than the star, and she began to speak to me sweet and low, with angelic voice, in her own tongue: 'O courteous Mantuan soul, of whom the fame yet lasteth in the world, and shall last so long as the world endureth! a friend of mine and not of fortune upon the desert hillside is so hindered on his road that he has turned for fear, and I am afraid, through that which I have heard of him in heaven, lest already he be so astray that I may have risen late to his succor. Now do thou move, and with thy speech ornate, and with whatever is needful for his deliverance, assist him so that I may be consoled for him. I am Beatricè who make thee go. I come from a place whither I desire to return. Love moved me, and makes me speak. When I shall be before my Lord, I will commend thee often unto Him.' Then she was silent, and thereon I began: 'O Lady of Virtue, thou alone through whom the human race surpasseth all contained within that heaven which hath the smallest circles![2] so pleasing unto me is thy command that to obey it, were it already done, were slow to me. Thou hast no need further to

[1] In Limbo, neither in Hell nor Heaven.
[2] The heaven of the moon, nearest to the earth.

open unto me thy will; but tell me the cause why
thou guardest not thyself from descending down
here into this centre, from the ample place whither
thou burnest to return.' 'Since thou wishest to
know so inwardly, I will tell thee briefly,' she replied to me, 'wherefore I fear not to come here
within. One ought to fear those things only that
have power of doing harm, the others not, for they
are not dreadful. I am made by God, thanks be
to Him, such that your misery toucheth me not,
nor doth the flame of this burning assail me. A
gentle Lady [1] is in heaven who hath pity for this
hindrance whereto I send thee, so that stern judgment there above she breaketh. She summoned
Lucia in her request, and said, " Thy faithful one
now hath need of thee, and unto thee I commend
him." Lucia, the foe of every cruel one, rose and
came to the place where I was, seated with the ancient Rachel. She said, " Beatrice, true praise of
God, why dost thou not succor him who so loved
thee that for thee he came forth from the vulgar
throng? Dost thou not hear the pity of his plaint?
Dost thou not see the death that combats him beside the stream whereof the sea hath no vaunt?"
In the world never were persons swift to seek
their good, and to fly their harm, as I, after these
words were uttered, came here below, from my

[1] The Virgin.

blessed seat, putting my trust in thy upright speech, which honors thee and them who have heard it.' After she had said this to me, weeping she turned her lucent eyes, whereby she made me more speedy in coming. And I came to thee as she willed. Thee have I delivered from that wild beast that took from thee the short ascent of the beautiful mountain. What is it then? Why, why dost thou hold back? why dost thou harbor such cowardice in thy heart? why hast thou not daring and boldness, since three blessed Ladies care for thee in the court of Heaven, and my speech pledges thee such good?"

As flowerets, bent and closed by the chill of night, after the sun shines on them straighten themselves all open on their stem, so I became with my weak virtue, and such good daring hastened to my heart that I began like one enfranchised : " Oh compassionate she who succored me ! and thou courteous who didst speedily obey the true words that she addressed to thee ! Thou by thy words hast so disposed my heart with desire of going, that I have returned unto my first intent. Go on now, for one sole will is in us both : Thou Leader, thou Lord, and thou Master." Thus I said to him ; and when he had moved on, I entered along the deep and savage road.

CANTO III.

The gate of Hell. Virgil leads Dante in. The punishment of the neither good nor bad. Acheron, and the sinners on its bank. Charon. Earthquake. Dante swoons.

"THROUGH me is the way into the woeful city; through me is the way into eternal woe; through me is the way among the lost people. Justice moved my lofty maker: the divine Power, the supreme Wisdom and the primal Love made me. Before me were no things created, unless eternal, and I eternal last. Leave every hope, ye who enter!"

These words of color obscure I saw written at the top of a gate; whereat I, "Master, their meaning is dire to me."

And he to me, like one who knew, "Here it behoves to leave every fear; it behoves that all cowardice should here be dead. We have come to the place where I have told thee that thou shalt see the woeful people, who have lost the good of the understanding."

And when he had put his hand on mine, with a glad countenance, wherefrom I took courage, he brought me within the secret things. Here sighs, laments, and deep wailings were resounding through the starless air; wherefore at first I wept thereat. Strange tongues, horrible cries, words of woe, accents of anger, voices high and hoarse, and sounds of hands with them, were making a tumult which whirls forever in that air dark without change, like the sand when the whirlwind breathes.

And I, who had my head girt with horror, said, "Master, what is it that I hear? and what folk are they who seem in woe so vanquished?"

And he to me, "This miserable measure the wretched souls maintain of those who lived without infamy and without praise. Mingled are they with that caitiff choir of the angels, who were not rebels, nor were faithful to God, but were for themselves. The heavens chased them out in order to be not less beautiful, nor doth the depth of Hell receive them, because the damned would have some glory from them."

And I, "Master, what is so grievous to them, that makes them lament so bitterly?"

He answered, "I will tell thee very briefly. These have no hope of death; and their blind life is so debased, that they are envious of every other lot. Fame of them the world permitteth not to be; mercy and justice disdain them. Let us not speak of them, but do thou look and pass on."

And I, who was gazing, saw a banner, that whirling ran so swiftly that it seemed to me to scorn all repose, and behind it came so long a train of folk, that I could never have believed death had undone so many. After I had distinguished some among them, I saw and knew the shade of him who made, through cowardice, the great refusal.[1] At once I understood and was certain, that this was the sect of the caitiffs displeasing unto God, and unto his enemies. These wretches, who never were alive, were naked, and much stung by gad-flies and by wasps that were there. These streaked their faces with blood, which, mingled with tears, was harvested at their feet by loathsome worms.

And when I gave myself to looking onward, I saw people on the bank of a great river; wherefore I said, "Master, now grant to me that I may know who these are, and what rule makes them appear so ready to pass over, as I discern through the faint light." And he to me, "The things will be clear to thee, when we shall set our steps on the sad marge of Acheron." Then with eyes bashful and cast down, fearing lest my speech had been irksome to him, far as to the river I refrained from speaking.

And lo! coming toward us in a boat, an old man, white with ancient hair, crying, "Woe to you, wicked souls! hope not ever to see Heaven! I come to carry you to the other bank, into eternal

---

[1] Who is intended by these words is uncertain.

darkness, to heat and frost. And thou who art there, living soul, depart from these that are dead." But when he saw that I did not depart, he said, " By another way, by other ports thou shalt come to the shore, not here, for passage; it behoves that a lighter bark bear thee." [1]

And my Leader to him, " Charon, vex not thyself, it is thus willed there where is power to do that which is willed; and farther ask not." Then the fleecy cheeks were quiet of the pilot of the livid marsh, who round about his eyes had wheels of flame.

But those souls, who were weary and naked, changed color, and gnashed their teeth soon as they heard his cruel words. They blasphemed God and their parents, the human race, the place, the time and the seed of their sowing and of their birth. Then, bitterly weeping, they drew back all of them together to the evil bank, that waits for every man who fears not God. Charon the demon, with eyes of glowing coal, beckoning them, collects them all; he beats with his oar whoever lingers.

As in autumn the leaves fall off one after the other, till the bough sees all its spoils upon the earth, in like wise the evil seed of Adam throw themselves from that shore one by one at signals,

[1] The boat that bears the souls to Purgatory. Charon recognizes that Dante is not among the damned.

as the bird at his call. Thus they go over the dusky wave, and before they have landed on the farther side, already on this a new throng is gathered.

"My son," said the courteous Master, "those who die in the wrath of God, all meet together here from every land. And they are eager to pass over the stream, for the divine justice spurs them, so that fear is turned to desire. This way a good soul never passes ; and therefore if Charon snarleth at thee, thou now mayest well know what his speech signifies."

This ended, the dark plain trembled so mightily, that the memory of the terror even now bathes me with sweat. The tearful land gave forth a wind that flashed a vermilion light which vanquished every sense of mine, and I fell as a man whom slumber seizes.

CANTO IV.

The further side of Acheron. Virgil leads Dante intc Limbo, the First Circle of Hell, containing the spirits of those who lived virtuously but without Christianity. Greeting of Virgil by his fellow poets. They enter a castle, where are the shades of ancient worthies. Virgil and Dante depart.

A HEAVY thunder broke the deep sleep in my head, so that I started up like a person who by force is wakened. And risen erect, I moved my rested eye round about, and looked fixedly to distinguish the place where I was. True it is, that I found myself on the verge of the valley of the woeful abyss that gathers in thunder of infinite wailings. Dark, profound it was, and cloudy, so that though I fixed my sight on the bottom I did not discern anything there.

"Now we descend down here into the blind world," began the Poet all deadly pale, "I will be first, and thou shalt be second."

And I, who had observed his color, said, "How shall I come, if thou fearest, who art wont to be a comfort to my doubting?" And he to me, "The anguish of the folk who are down here depicts upon my face that pity which thou takest for fear. Let us go on, for the long way urges us."

So he set forth, and so he made me enter within the first circle that girds the abyss. Here, so far as could be heard, there was no plaint but that of sighs which 'made the eternal air to tremble: this came of the woe without torments felt by the crowds, which were many and great, of infants and of women and of men.

The good Master to me, " Thou dost not ask what spirits are these that thou seest. Now I would have thee know, before thou goest farther, that they sinned not ; and if they have merits it sufficeth not, because they had not baptism, which is part of the faith that thou believest; and if they were before Christianity, they did not duly worship God : and of such as these am I myself. Through such defects, and not through other guilt, are we lost, and only so far harmed that without hope we live in desire."

Great woe seized me at my heart when I heard him, because I knew that people of much worth were suspended in that limbo. " Tell me, my Master, tell me, Lord," began I, with wish to be assured of that faith which vanquishes every error,[1] " did ever any one who afterwards was blessed go

[1] Wishing especially to be assured in regard to the descent of Christ into Hell.

out from here, either by his own or by another's merit?" And he, who understood my covert speech, answered, "I was new in this state when I saw a Mighty One come hither crowned with sign of victory. He drew out hence the shade of the first parent, of Abel his son, and that of Noah, of Moses the law-giver and obedient, Abraham the patriarch, and David the King, Israel with his father, and with his offspring, and with Rachel, for whom he did so much, and others many; and He made them blessed : and I would have thee know that before these, human spirits were not saved."

We ceased not going on because he spoke, but all the while were passing through the wood, the wood I mean of crowded spirits. Nor yet had our way been long from where I slept, when I saw a fire, that conquered a hemisphere of darkness. We were still a little distant from it, yet not so far that I could not partially discern that honorable folk possessed that place. "O thou that honorest both science and art, these, who are they, that have such honor that from the condition of the others it sets them apart?" And he to me, "The honorable fame of them which resounds above in thy life wins grace in heaven that so advances them." At this a voice was heard by me, "Honor the loftiest Poet! his shade returns that was departed." When the voice had ceased and was quiet, I saw four great shades coming to us : they had a semblance neither sad nor glad. The good Master began to say, " Look at him with that sword in hand who cometh before the three, even as lord. He is Homer, the sovereign poet; the next who comes is Horace, the satirist; Ovid is the third, and the last is Lucan. Since each shares with me the name that the single voice sounded, they do me honor, and in that do well."

Thus I saw assembled the fair school of that Lord of the loftiest song which above the others as an eagle flies. After they had discoursed somewhat together, they turned to me with sign of salutation; and my Master smiled thereat. And far more of honor yet they did me, for they made me of their band, so that I was the sixth amid so much wit. Thus we went on as far as the light, speaking things concerning which silence is becoming, even as was speech there where I was.

We came to the foot of a noble castle, seven times circled by high walls, defended round about by a fair streamlet. This we passed as if hard ground; through seven gates I entered with these sages; we came to a meadow of fresh verdure. People were there with eyes slow and grave, of great authority in their looks; they spake seldom, and with soft voices. Thus we drew apart, on one side, into a place open, luminous, and high, so that they all could be seen. There opposite upon the green enamel were shown to me the great spirits, whom to have seen I inwardly exalt myself.

I saw Electra with many companions, among whom I knew both Hector and Æneas, Cæsar in armor, with his gerfalcon eyes; I saw Camilla and Penthesilea on the other side, and I saw the King Latinus, who was seated with Lavinia his daughter. I saw that Brutus who drove out Tarquin; Lucretia, Julia, Marcia, and Cornelia; and alone, apart, I saw the Saladin. When I raised my brow a little more, I saw the Master of those who know, seated amid the philosophic family; all regard him, all do him honor. Here I saw both Socrates and Plato, who before the others stand nearest to him; Democritus, who ascribes the world to chance; Diogenes, Anaxagoras, and Thales, Empedocles, Heraclitus, and Zeno; and I saw the good collector of the qualities, Dioscorides, I mean; and I saw Orpheus, Tully, and Linus, and moral Seneca, Euclid the geometer, and Ptolemy, Hippocrates, Avicenna, Galen, and Averrhoës, who made the great comment. I cannot report of all in full, because the long theme so drives me that many times speech comes short of fact.

The company of six is reduced to two. By another way the wise guide leads me, out from the quiet, into the air that trembles, and I come into a region where is nothing that can give light.

CANTO V.

The Second Circle, that of Carnal Sinners. — Minos. — Shades renowned of old. — Francesca da Rimini.

THUS I descended from the first circle down into the second, which girdles less space, and so much more woe that it goads to wailing. There abides Minos horribly, and snarls; he examines the sins at the entrance; he judges, and he sends according as he entwines himself. I mean, that, when the miscreant spirit comes there before him, it confesses itself wholly, and that discerner of sins sees what place of Hell is for it; he girdles himself with his tail so many times as the degrees he wills it should be sent down. Always before him stand many of them. They go, in turn, each to the judgment; they speak, and hear, and then are whirled below.

"O thou that comest to the woeful inn," said Minos to me, when he saw me, leaving the act of so great an office, " beware how thou enterest, and to whom thou trustest thyself; let not the amplitude of the entrance deceive thee." And my Leader to him, " Why then dost thou cry out ? Hinder not his fated going; thus is it willed there where is power to do that which is willed; and ask thou no more."

Now the woeful notes begin to make themselves heard ; now am I come where much lamentation smites me. I had come into a place mute of all light, that bellows as the sea does in a tempest, if it be combated by opposing winds. The infernal hurricane that never rests carries along the spirits in its rapine; whirling and smiting it molests them. When they arrive before its rushing blast, here are shrieks, and bewailing, and lamenting; here they blaspheme the power divine. I understood that to such torment are condemned the carnal sinners who subject reason to appetite. And as their wings bear along the starlings in the cold season in a troop large and full, so that blast the evil spirits; hither, thither, down, up it carries them; no hope ever comforts them, not of repose, but even of less pain.

And as the cranes go singing their lays, making in air a long line of themselves, so saw I come, uttering wails, shades borne along by the aforesaid strife. Wherefore I said, " Master, who are those folk whom the black air so castigates?" "The first of these of whom thou wishest to have knowledge," said he to me then, " was empress of many tongues. To the vice of luxury was she so aban-

doned that lust she made licit in her law, to take
away the blame she had incurred. She is Semi-
ramis, of whom it is read that she succeeded Ninus
and had been his spouse; she held the land which
the Soldan rules. That other is she who, for love,
killed herself, and broke faith to the ashes of Si-
chaeus. Next is Cleopatra, the luxurious. See
Helen, for whom so long a time of ill revolved;
and see the great Achilles, who at the end fought
with love. See Paris, Tristan, — " and more than
a thousand shades he showed me with his finger,
and named them, whom love had parted from our
life.

After I had heard my Teacher name the dames of
eld and the cavaliers, pity overcame me, and I was
well nigh bewildered. I began, " Poet, willingly
would I speak with those two that go together, and
seem to be so light upon the wind." And he to
me, " Thou shalt see when they shall be nearer to
us, and do thou then pray them by that love which
leads them, and they will come." Soon as the wind
sways them toward us I lifted my voice, " O weary
souls, come speak to us, if One forbid it not."

As doves, called by desire, with wings open and
steady, fly through the air to their sweet nest, borne
by their will, these issued from the troop where
Dido is, coming to us through the malign air, so
strong was the compassionate cry.

"O living creature, gracious and benign, that goest through the lurid air visiting us who stained the world blood-red, — if the King of the universe were a friend we would pray Him for thy peace, since thou hast pity on our perverse ill. Of what it pleaseth thee to hear, and what to speak, we will hear and we will speak to you, while the wind, as now, is hushed for us. The city where I was born sits upon the sea-shore, where the Po, with its followers, descends to have peace. Love, that on gentle heart quickly lays hold, seized him for the fair person that was taken from me, and the mode still hurts me. Love, which absolves no loved one from loving, seized me for the pleasing of him so strongly that, as thou seest, it does not even now abandon me. Love brought us to one death. Caina awaits him who quenched our life." These words were borne to us from them.

Soon as I had heard those injured souls I bowed my face, and held it down, until the Poet said to me, "What art thou thinking?" When I replied, I began, "Alas! how many sweet thoughts, how great desire, led these unto the woeful pass." Then I turned me again to them, and I spoke, and began, "Francesca, thy torments make me sad and piteous to weeping. But tell me, at the time of the sweet sighs by what and how did love concede to you to know the dubious desires?" And she to me, " There is no greater woe than in misery to remember the happy time, and that thy Teacher knows. But if to know the first root of our love thou hast so great a longing, I will do like one who weeps and tells.

" We were reading one day, for delight, of Lancelot, how love constrained him. We were alone and without any suspicion. Many times that reading made us lift our eyes, and took the color from our faces, but only one point was that which overcame us. When we read of the longed-for smile being kissed by such a lover, this one, who never from me shall be divided, kissed my mouth all trembling. Galahaut was the book, and he who wrote it. That day we read in it no farther." [1]

While one spirit said this the other was weeping so that through pity I swooned, as if I had been dying, and fell as a dead body falls.

---

[1] In the Romance, it was Galahaut that prevailed on Guinevere to give a kiss to Lancelot.

CANTO VI.

The Third Circle, that of the Gluttonous. — Cerberus. — Ciacco.

WHEN the mind returned, which closed itself before the pity of these two kinsfolk, that had all confounded me with sadness, new torments and new tormented souls I see around me wherever I move, and howsoever I turn, and wherever I gaze.

I am in the third circle, that of the rain eternal, accursed, cold, and heavy. Its rule and quality are never new. Coarse hail, and foul water and snow pour down through the tenebrous air; the earth that receives them stinks. Cerberus, a beast cruel and monstrous, with three throats barks dog-like above the people that are here submerged. He has vermilion eyes, and a greasy and black beard, and a big belly, and hands armed with claws: he tears the spirits, flays them, and rends them. The rain makes them howl like dogs; of one of their sides they make a screen for the other; the profane wretches often turn themselves.

When Cerberus, the great worm, observed us

he opened his mouths, and showed his fangs to us; not a limb had he that he kept quiet. And my Leader opened wide his hands, took some earth, and with full fists threw it into the ravenous gullets. As the dog that barking craves, and becomes quiet when he bites his food, and is intent and fights only to devour it, such became those filthy faces of the demon Cerberus, who so thunders at the souls that they would fain be deaf.

We were passing over the shades whom the heavy rain subdues, and were setting our feet upon their vain show that seems a body. They all of them lay upon the ground, except one who raised himself to sit, quickly as he saw us passing before him. "O thou who art led through this Hell," he said to me, "recognize me, if thou canst; thou wast made before I was unmade." And I to him, "The anguish which thou hast perchance withdraws thee from my memory, so that it seems not that I ever saw thee. But tell me who thou art, that in a place so woeful art set, and with such a punishment, that if any other is greater none is so displeasing." And he to me, "Thy city which is so full of envy, that already the sack runs over, held me in it, in the serene life. You citizens called me Ciacco;[1] for the damnable sin of gluttony, as thou seest, I am broken by the rain. And I, wretched soul, am

---

[1] Ciacco, in popular speech, signifies a *hog.*

not alone, for all these endure like punishment, for
like sin," and more he said not.   I answered him,
"Ciacco, thy trouble so weighs upon me, that it in-
vites me to weeping; but tell me, if thou canst, to
what will come the citizens of the divided city; if
any one in it is just; and tell me the reason why
such great discord has assailed it."

And he to me, "After long contention they will
come to blood, and the savage party will chase out
the other with great injury.   Thereafter within
three suns it behoves this to fall, and the other
to surmount through the force of one who even
now is tacking.   It will hold high its front long
time, keeping the other under heavy burdens, however it may lament and be shamed thereat.   Two
men are just, but there they are not heeded; Pride,
Envy, Avarice are the three sparks that have inflamed their hearts."[1]   Here he set end unto the
lamentable sound.

And I to him, "Still I would that thou teach me,
and that of more speech thou make a gift to me.
Farinata and the Tegghiaio who were so worthy,
Jacopo Rusticucci, Arrigo, and the Mosca, and the

[1] This prophecy relates to the dissensions and violence of the
parties of the Whites and the Blacks by which Florence was rent.
The "savage party" was that of the Whites, who were mainly
Ghibellines.   The "one who even now is tacking" was the Pope,
Boniface VIII., who was playing fast and loose with both.   Who
the "two just men" were is unknown.

rest who set their minds on well-doing, tell me where they are, and cause that I may know them, for great desire constrains me to learn if Heaven sweeten them, or Hell envenom."

And he, " They are among the blacker souls : a different sin weighs them down to the bottom; if thou so far descendest, thou canst see them. But when thou shalt be in the sweet world I pray thee that thou bring me to the memory of others. More I say not to thee, and more I answer thee not." His straight eyes he twisted then awry, looked at me a little, and then bent his head, and fell with it level with the other blind.

And the Leader said to me, " He wakes no more this side the sound of the angelic trump. When the hostile Sovereign shall come, each one will find again his dismal tomb, will take again his flesh and his shape, will hear that which through eternity reëchoes."

Thus we passed along with slow steps through the foul mixture of the shades and of the rain, touching a little on the future life. Wherefore I said, " Master, these torments will they increase after the great sentence, or will they become less, or will they be just as burning ? " And he to me, " Return to thy science, which declares that the more perfect a thing is the more it feels the good, and so the pain. Though this accursed people never can attain to true perfection, it expects thereafter to be more than now."

We took a circling course along that road, speaking far more than I repeat ; and came to the point where the descent is.   Here we found Pluto,[1] the great enemy.

[1] Pluto appears here not as Hades, the god of the lower world, but in his character as the giver of wealth.

CANTO VII.

The Fourth Circle, that of the Avaricious and the Prodigal. — Pluto. — Fortune.

The Styx. — The Fifth Circle, that of the Wrathful and the Sullen.

"*Pape Satan, pape Satan aleppe,*" — began Pluto with his clucking voice. And that gentle Sage, who knew everything, said to comfort me, "Let not thy fear hurt thee; for whatso power he have shall not take from thee the descent of this rock." Then he turned to that swollen lip and said, "Be silent, accursed wolf! inwardly consume thyself with thine own rage: not without cause is this going to the abyss; it is willed on high, there where Michael did vengeance on the proud adultery."[1] As sails swollen by the wind fall in a heap when the mast snaps, so fell to earth the cruel beast.

Thus we descended into the fourth hollow, taking more of the woeful bank that gathers in the evil of the whole universe. Ah, Justice of God! Who heapeth up so many new travails and penalties as I saw? And why doth our sin so waste us? As

---

[1] Adultery, in the sense of infidelity to God.

doth the wave, yonder upon Charybdis, which is broken on that which it encounters, so it behoves that here the people counterdance.

Here saw I people more than elsewhere many, and from one side and the other with great howls rolling weights by force of chest. They struck against each other, and then just there each turned, rolling backward, crying, "Why keepest thou?" and "Why flingest thou away?" Thus they turned through the dark circle on either hand to the opposite point, still crying out their opprobrious verse; then each, when he had come through his half circle, wheeled round to the other joust.

And I, who had my heart well-nigh pierced through, said, "My Master, now declare to me what folk is this, and if all these tonsured ones on our left were clerks."

And he to me, "All of these were so asquint in mind in the first life that they made no spending there with measure. Clearly enough their voices bay it out, when they come to the two points of the circle where the contrary sin divides them. These were clerks who have no hairy covering on their head, and Popes and Cardinals, in whom avarice practices its excess."

And I, "Master, among such as these I ought surely to recognize some who were polluted with these evils."

And he to me, "Vain thought thou harborest; the undiscerning life that made them foul, to all recognition now makes them dim. Forever will they come to the two buttings; these will rise from the sepulchre with closed fist, and these with shorn hair. Ill-giving and ill-keeping have taken from them the fair world, and set them to this scuffle; such as it is, I adorn not words for it. Now canst thou, son, see the brief jest of the goods that are committed unto Fortune, for which the human race so scramble; for all the gold that is beneath the moon, or that ever was, of these weary souls could not make a single one repose."

" Master," said I to him, " now tell me further; this Fortune, on which thou touchest for me, what is it, that hath the goods of the world so in its clutches ? "

And he to me, " O creatures foolish, how great is that ignorance that harms you ! I would have thee now take in my judgment of her. He whose wisdom transcendeth all made the heavens, and gave them their guides, so that every part on every part doth shine, equally distributing the light. In like wise for the splendors of the world, He ordained a general ministress and guide, who should ever and anon transfer the vain goods from race to race, and from one blood to another, beyond the resistance of human wit. Wherefore one race rules, and the other languishes, pursuant to her judgment, which is occult as the snake in the grass. Your wisdom hath no withstanding of her : she provides, judges and maintains her realm, as theirs the other gods. Her permutations have no truce ; necessity compels her to be swift, so often cometh he who obtains a turn. This is she who is so set upon the cross, even by those who ought to give her praise, giving her blame amiss and ill report. But she is blessed and hears this not. With the other Primal Creatures glad she turns her sphere, and blessed she rejoices. But now let us descend to greater woe. Already every star sinks that was rising when I set out, and too long stay is forbidden."

We crossed the circle to the other bank, above a fount that boils and pours down through a cleft that proceeds from it. The water was far darker than perse ;[1] and we, in company with the dusky waves, entered down through a strange way. A marsh it makes, that is named Styx, this dismal little stream, when it has descended to the foot of the malign gray slopes. And I, who stood intent to gaze, saw muddy people in that swamp, all naked and with look of hurt. They were smiting each other, not only with hands, but with head, and with chest, and with feet, mangling one another piecemeal with their teeth.

[1] Purple-black.

The good Master said, " Son, now thou seest the souls of those whom anger overcame ; and likewise I would have thee believe for certain that beneath the water are folk who sigh, and make this water bubble at the surface, as thine eye tells thee wher- ever it turns. Fixed in the slime, they say, ' Sul- len were we in the sweet air that by the Sun is gladdened, bearing within ourselves the sluggish fume ; now we are sullen in the black mire.' This hymn they gurgle in their throats, for they cannot speak with entire words." [1]

Thus we circled a great arc of the foul fen, between the dry bank and the slough, with eyes turned on those who guzzle the mire. We came at length to the foot of a tower.

[1] The sin here punished is that known to the Middle Ages as *acedia*, or *accidie*, — slackness in good works, and spiritual gloom and despondency. In the Parson's Tale Chaucer says : " Envie and ire maken bitternesse in heart, which bitternesse is mother of accidie."

CANTO VIII.

The Fifth Circle. — Phlegyas and his boat. — Passage of
the Styx. — Filippo Argenti. — The City of Dis. — The
demons refuse entrance to the poets.

I SAY, continuing, that, long before we were at
the foot of the high tower, our eyes went upward
to its top because of two flamelets that we saw set
there, and another giving signal back from so far
that hardly could the eye reach it. And I turned
me to the Sea of all wisdom; I said, "This one,
what says it? and what answers that other fire?
and who are they that make it?" And he to me,
"Upon the foul waves already thou mayest discern that which is expected, if the fume of the
marsh hide it not from thee."

Bowstring never sped arrow from itself that ran
so swift a course through the air, as a very little
boat which I saw coming through the water toward
us at that instant, under the direction of a single
ferryman, who was crying out, "Art thou then
come, fell soul?"

"Phlegyas, Phlegyas, this time thou criest out in
vain," said my Lord; "longer thou shalt not have

us than only while crossing the slough." As one who listens to some great deceit that has been practiced on him, and then chafes at it, such became Phlegyas in his stifled anger.

My Leader descended into the bark and then he made me enter after him, and only when I was in did it seem laden. Soon as my Leader and I were in the boat, the antique prow goes its way, cutting more of the water than it is wont with others.

While we were running through the dead channel, before me showed himself one full of mud, and said, " Who art thou that comest before the hour ? " And I to him, " If I come I stay not; but thou, who art thou that art become so foul ? " He answered, " Thou seest that I am one who weeps." And I to him, " With weeping and with wailing, accursed spirit, do thou remain, for I know thee although thou art all filthy." Then he stretched to the boat both his hands, whereat the wary Master thrust him back, saying, " Begone there, with the other dogs ! " Then with his arms he clasped my neck, kissed my face, and said, " Disdainful soul, blessed be she who bore thee ! This one was an arrogant person in the world; no goodness is there that adorns his memory; therefore is his shade so furious here. How many now up there are held great kings who shall stand here like swine in mire, leaving of themselves horrible dispraises."

And I, "Master, I should much like to see him ducked in this broth before we depart from the lake." And he to me, " Ere the shore allows thee to see it thou shalt be satisfied ; it will be fitting that thou enjoy such a desire." After this a little I saw such rending of him by the muddy folk that I still praise God therefor, and thank Him for it. All cried, " At Filippo Argenti ! " and the raging Florentine spirit turned upon himself with his teeth. Here we left him ; so that I tell no more of him.

But on my ears there smote a wailing, whereat forward intent I open wide my eye. And the good Master said, " Now, son, the city draws near that is named Dis, with its heavy citizens, with its great throng." And I, " Master, already in the valley therewithin I clearly discern its mosques vermilion, as if issuing from fire." And he said to me, " The eternal fire that blazes within them displays them red as thou seest in this nether Hell."

We at last arrived within the deep ditches that encompass that disconsolate city. The walls seemed to me to be of iron. Not without first making a great circuit did we come to a place where the ferryman loudly shouted to us, " Out with you, here is the entrance."

Upon the gates I saw more than a thousand of those rained down from heaven who angrily were saying, "Who is this, that without death goes through the realm of the dead folk?" And my wise Master made a sign of wishing to speak secretly with them. Then they shut in a little their great scorn, and said, "Come thou alone, and let him be gone who so boldly entered on this realm. Alone let him return on the mad path : let him try if he can; for thou, who hast escorted him through so dark a region, shalt remain here."

Think, Reader, if I was discomforted at the sound of the accursed words, for I did not believe ever to return hither. [1]

" O my dear Leader, who more than seven times hast renewed assurance in me, and drawn me from deep peril that stood confronting me, leave me not," said I, "thus undone ; and, if the going farther onward be denied us, let us together retrace our footprints quickly." And that Lord who had led me thither said to me, " Fear not, for no one can take from us our onward way, by Such an one it is given to us. But here await me, and comfort thy dejected spirit and feed on good hope, for I will not leave thee in the nether world."

So the sweet Father goes away, and here abandons me, and I remain in suspense ; and yes and no contend within my head. I could not hear what he set forth to them, but he had not staid there long

[1] To this world.

with them, when each ran vying back within. These our adversaries closed the gates on the breast of my Lord, who remained without, and returned to me with slow steps.   He held his eyes upon the ground, and his brow was shorn of all hardihood, and he said in sighs, "Who hath denied to me the houses of woe?"   And he said to me, " Thou, because I am wroth, be not dismayed, for I shall win the strife, whoever circle round within for the defence.   This their insolence is not new, for of old they used it at a less secret gate, which still is found without a bolt.   Above it thou didst see the dead inscription; and already on this side of it descends the steep, passing without escort through the circles, One such that by him the city shall be opened to us."

CANTO IX.

The City of Dis. — Erichtho. — The Three Furies. — The Heavenly Messenger. — The Sixth Circle, that of the Heresiarchs.

THAT color which cowardice painted outwardly on me when I saw my Guide turn back, repressed more speedily his own new color. He stopped attentive, like a man that listens, for the eye could not lead him far through the black air, and through the dense fog.

"Yet it must be for us to win the fight," began he, "unless — Such an one offered herself to us.[1] Oh how slow it seems till Some one here arrive!"[2]

I saw well how he covered up the beginning with the rest that came after, which were words different from the first. But nevertheless his speech gave me fear, because I drew his broken phrase perchance to a worse meaning than it held.

"Into this depth of the dismal shell does any one ever descend from the first grade who has for

[1] Beatrice.

[2] The messenger from Heaven, referred to in the last verses of the last canto.

penalty only hope cut off?"[1] This question I put,
and he answered me, "Seldom it happens that any
one of us maketh the journey on which I am going.
It is true that another time I was conjured down
here by that cruel Erichtho who was wont to call
back shades into their bodies. Short while had my
flesh been bare of me, when she made me enter
within that wall in order to drag out for her a
spirit from the circle of Judas. That is the lowest
place, and the darkest, and the farthest from the
Heaven that encircles all. Well do I know the
road : therefore assure thyself. This marsh which
breathes out the great stench girds round about the
woeful city wherein now we cannot enter without
anger."

And more he said, but I hold it not in mind because my eye had wholly attracted me toward the
high tower with the ruddy summit, where in an instant were uprisen suddenly three infernal furies,
stained with blood, who had the limbs of women
and their action, and were girt with greenest hy-
dras. Little serpents and cerastes they had for
hair, wherewith their savage brows were bound.

And he, who well knew the handmaids of the
queen of the eternal lamentation, said to me, "Behold the fell Erinnyes; this is Megaera on the

[1] Dante asks for assurance that Virgil, whose station is in
Limbo, "the first grade," knows the way.

left side, she who weeps on the right is Alecto, Tisiphone is in the middle," and therewith he was silent.

With her nails each was tearing her breast, they beat themselves with their hands, and cried out so loud that I pressed close to the Poet through dread. "Let Medusa come, so we will make him of stone," they all said, looking down. " Ill was it we avenged not on Theseus his assault."

"Turn thy back, and keep thy sight closed, for if the Gorgon show herself, and thou shouldest see her, no return upward would there ever be." Thus said the Master, and he himself turned me, and did not so trust to my hands that with his own he did not also blindfold me.

O ye who have sound understanding, regard the doctrine that is hidden under the veil of the strange verses.

And already was coming across the turbid waves a tumult of a sound full of terror at which both the shores trembled. Not otherwise it was than of a wind, impetuous through the opposing heats, that strikes the forest, and without any stay shatters the branches, beats down and carries them away ; forward, laden with dust, it goes superb, and makes the wild beasts and the shepherds fly.

My eyes he loosed, and said, " Now direct the nerve of sight across the ancient scum, there yonder where that fume is most bitter."

As frogs before the hostile snake all scatter through the water, till each huddles on the ground, I saw more than a thousand destroyed souls flying thus before one, who at the ford was passing over the Styx with dry feet. From his face he removed that thick air, waving his left hand oft before him, and only with that trouble seemed he weary. Well I perceived that he was sent from Heaven, and I turned me to the Master, and he made sign that I should stand quiet and bow down unto him. Ah, how full of disdain he seemed to me! He reached the gate and with a little rod he opened it, for there was no withstanding.

"O outcasts from Heaven, folk despised," began he upon the horrible threshold, "wherefore is this overweening harbored in you? Why do ye kick against that will from which its end can never be cut short, and which many a time hath increased your grief? What avails it to butt against the fates? Your Cerberus, if ye remember well, still bears his chin and his throat peeled for that." Then he turned back upon the filthy road and said no word to us, but wore the semblance of a man whom other care constrains and stings, than that of him who is before him.

And we moved our feet toward the city, confident after his holy words. Within we entered without any strife, and I, who had desire to observe the condition which such a stronghold locks in, when I was within, sent my eyes round about; and I see on every hand a great plain full of woe and of cruel torment.

As at Arles, where the Rhone stagnates, as at Pola, near the Quarnaro that shuts in Italy and bathes its borders, sepulchres make all the place uneven; so did they here on every side, saving that the manner was more bitter here; for among the tombs flames were scattered, by which they were so intensely kindled that no art requires iron more so. All their lids were lifted; and such dire laments were issuing forth from them as truly seemed of wretches and of sufferers.

And I, " Master, who are these folk that, buried within those coffers, make themselves heard with their woeful sighs?" And he to me, " Here are the heresiarchs with their followers of every sect, and the tombs are much more laden than thou thinkest. Like with like is buried here, and the monuments are more and less hot."

And when he to the right hand had turned, we passed between the torments and the high battlements.

CANTO X.

Now along a narrow path between the wall of the city and the torments my Master goeth on, and I behind his shoulders.

" O Virtue supreme," I began, " that through the impious circles turnest me, according to thy pleasure, speak to me and satisfy my desires. The folk that are lying in the sepulchres, can they be seen? All the lids are now lifted, and no one keepeth guard." And he to me, " All shall be locked in when from Jehoshaphat they shall here return with the bodies which they have left on earth. Upon this side Epicurus with all his followers, who make the soul mortal with the body, have their burial place. Therefore as to the demand that thou makest of me, thou shalt soon be satisfied here within; and also as to the desire concerning which thou art silent to me." And I, " Good Leader, I hold not my heart hidden from thee except in order to speak little; and not only now to that hast thou disposed me."

" O Tuscan, who through the city of fire alive art going, speaking thus modestly, may it please thee to stop in this place. Thy speech makes man-ifest that thou art native of that noble fatherland to which perchance I was too molestful." Sud-denly this sound issued from one of the coffers, wherefore I drew, in fear, a little nearer to my Leader. And he said to me, " Turn, what dost thou? Behold Farinata who hath uprisen; thou shalt see him all from the girdle up."

I had already fixed my face on his, and he straightened himself up with breast and front as though he had Hell in great scorn. And the bold and ready hands of my Leader pushed me among the sepulchres to him, saying, " Let thy words be choice."

When I was at the foot of his tomb, he looked at me a little, and then, as though disdainful, asked me, " Who were thy ancestors?" I, who was de-sirous to obey, concealed them not, but disclosed them all to him; whereon he raised his brows a lit-tle up, then said, " Fiercely were they adverse to me, and to my fathers, and to my party, so that twice I scattered them."[1] " If they were driven out, they returned from every side," replied I to him, " both one and the other time, but yours have not learned well that art."

[1] Dante's ancestors were Guelphs.

Then there arose, to view uncovered down to the chin, a shade at the side of this one; I think that it had risen on its knees. Round about me it looked, as if it had desire to see if another were with me, but when its expectancy was quite extinct, weeping it said, "If through this blind dungeon thou goest through loftiness of genius, my son, where is he? and why is he not with thee?" And I to him, "Of myself I come not; he who waits yonder leads me through here, whom perchance your Guido held in scorn." [1]

His words and the mode of the punishment had already read to me the name of this one, wherefore my answer was so full.

Suddenly straightening up, he cried, "How didst thou say, 'he held'? lives he not still? doth not the sweet light strike his eyes?" When he took note of some delay that I made before answering, he fell again supine, and forth appeared no more.

But that other magnanimous one, at whose instance I had stayed, changed not aspect, nor moved his neck, nor bent his side. "And if," he said, continuing his first words, "they have ill learned that art, it torments me more than this bed. But the face of the lady who ruleth here will not be

---

[1] Guido Cavalcanti was charged with the same sin of unbelief as his father. Dante regards this as a sin specially contrary to right reason, typified by Virgil.

rekindled fifty times ere thou shalt know how much
that art weighs. And, so mayest thou return unto
the sweet world, tell me wherefore is that people so
pitiless against my race in its every law?" Then
I to him, "The rout and the great carnage that
colored the Arbia red cause such orison to be made
in our temple." After he had, sighing, shaken
his head, "In that I was not alone," he said, "nor
surely without cause would I have moved with
the rest; but I was alone, — there [1] where it was
agreed by every one to lay Florence waste, — he
who defended her with open face." "Ah! so hereafter may your seed repose," I prayed to him,
"loose for me that knot, which here has entangled
my judgment. It seems, if I rightly hear, that
ye foresee that which time is bringing with him,
and as to the present have another way." "We
see," he said, "like those who have feeble light,
the things that are far from us, so much still shin-
eth on us the supreme Leader; when they draw
near, or are, our intelligence is all vain, and, if
some one report not to us, we know nothing of your
human state. Therefore thou canst comprehend
that our knowledge will be utterly dead from that
moment when the gate of the future shall be
closed." Then, as compunctious for my fault, I
said, "Now wilt thou therefore tell that fallen one

[1] At Empoli, in 1260, after the defeat of the Florentine Guelphs
at Montaperti on the Arbia.

that his son is still conjoined with the living, and if just now I was dumb to answer, make him know that I was so because I was still thinking in that error which you have solved for me." [1]

And now my Master was calling me back, wherefore I prayed the spirit more hastily that he would tell me who was with him. He said to me, " Here with more than a thousand do I lie; here within is the second Frederick and the Cardinal,[2] and of the others I am silent."

Thereon he hid himself; and I toward the ancient Poet turned my steps, reflecting on that speech which seemed hostile to me. He moved on, and then, thus going, he said to me, " Why art thou so distraught?" And I satisfied his demand. "Let thy memory preserve that which thou hast heard against thyself," commanded me that Sage, "and now attend to this," and he raised his finger. "When thou shalt be in presence of the sweet radiance of her whose beautiful eye sees everything, from her thou shalt learn the journey of thy life." Then to the left he turned his step.

We left the wall, and went toward the middle by a path which strikes into a valley that even up there its stench made displeasing.

---

[1] Guido Cavalcanti died in August, 1300; his death, being near at hand at the time of Dante's journey, was not known to his father.

[2] Ottaviano degli Ubaldini, a fierce Ghibelline, who was reported as saying, "If there be a soul I have lost it for the Ghibellines."

CANTO XI.

The Sixth Circle : Heretics. — Tomb of Pope Anastasius. — Discourse of Virgil on the divisions of the lower Hell.

UPON the edge of a high bank formed by great rocks broken in a circle, we came above a more cruel pen. And here, because of the horrible excess of the stench that the deep abyss throws out, we drew aside behind the lid of a great tomb, whereon I saw an inscription which said, "Pope Anastasius I hold, he whom Photinus drew from the right way."

"Our descent must needs be slow so that the sense may first accustom itself a little to the dismal blast, and then will be no heed of it." Thus the Master, and I said to him, "Some compensation do thou find that the time pass not lost." And he, "Behold, I am thinking of that. My son, within these rocks," he began to say, "are three circlets from grade to grade like those thou leavest. All are full of accursed spirits ; but, in order that hereafter sight only may suffice thee, hear how and wherefore they are in constraint.

"Of every malice that wins hate in heaven injury is the end, and every such end afflicts others either by force or by fraud. But because fraud is the peculiar sin of man, it most displeaseth God; and therefore the fraudulent are the lower, and more woe assails them.

"The first circle [1] is wholly of the violent; but because violence can be done to three persons, in three rounds it is divided and constructed. Unto God, unto one's self, unto one's neighbor may violence be done; I mean unto them and unto their belongings, as thou shalt hear in plain discourse. By violence death and grievous wounds are inflicted on one's neighbor; and on his substance ruins, burnings, and harmful robberies. Wherefore homicides, and every one who smites wrongfully, devastators and freebooters, all of them the first round torments, in various troops.

"Man may lay violent hands upon himself and on his goods; and, therefore, in the second round must needs repent without avail whoever deprives himself of your world, gambles away and squanders his property, and laments there where he ought to be joyous.[2]

"Violence may be done to the Deity, by denying and blaspheming Him in heart, and despising nature and His bounty: and therefore the smallest

---

[1] The first circle below, the seventh in the order of Hell.

[2] Laments on earth because of violence done to what should have made him happy.

round seals with its signet both Sodom and Cahors, and him who despising God speaks from his heart.

"Fraud, by which every conscience is bitten, man may practice on one that confides in him, or on one that owns no confidence. This latter mode seemeth to destroy only the bond of love that nature makes; wherefore in the second circle [1] nestle hypocrisy, flatteries, and sorcerers, falsity, robbery, and simony, panders, barrators, and such like filth.

"By the other mode that love is forgotten which nature makes, and also that which is thereafter added, whereby special confidence is created. Hence, in the smallest circle, where is the centre of the universe, on which Dis sits, whoso betrays is consumed forever."

And I, "Master, full clearly doth thy discourse proceed, and full well divides this pit, and the people that possess it; but, tell me, they of the fat marsh, and they whom the wind drives, and they whom the rain beats, and they who encounter with such sharp tongues, why are they not punished within the ruddy city if God be wroth with them? and if he be not so, why are they in such plight?"

And he said to me, "Wherefore so wanders thine understanding beyond its wont? or thy mind, where else is it gazing? Dost thou not remember those words with which thine Ethics treats in full of the

[1] The second circle below, the eighth in the order of Hell.

three dispositions that Heaven abides not; incontinence, malice, and mad bestiality, and how
incontinence less offends God, and incurs less
blame?[1] If thou considerest well this doctrine,
and bringest to mind who are those that up above,
outside,[2] suffer punishment, thou wilt see clearly
why from these felons they are divided, and why
less wroth the divine vengeance hammers them."

"O Sun that healest every troubled vision, thou
dost content me so, when thou explainest, that
doubt, not less than knowledge, pleaseth me; yet
return a little back," said I, "there where thou
saidst that usury offends the Divine Goodness, and
loose the knot."

"Philosophy," he said to me, "points out to him
who understands it, not only in one part alone, how
Nature takes her course from the Divine Intellect
and from its art. And if thou note thy Physics[3]
well thou wilt find after not many pages that your
art follows her so far as it can, as the disciple does
the master, so that your art is as it were grand-
child of God. By means of these two, if thou
bringest to mind Genesis at its beginning, it behoves mankind to obtain their livelihood and
to thrive. But because the usurer takes another

[1] Aristotle, *Ethics*, vii. 1.
[2] Outside the walls of the city of Dis.
[3] Aristotle, *Physics*, ii. 2.

course, he despises Nature in herself, and in her
follower, since upon other thing he sets his hope.
But follow me now, for to go on pleaseth me ; for
the Fishes are gliding on the horizon, and the
Wain lies quite over Corus,[1] and far yonder is
the way down the cliff."

[1] The time indicated is about 4, or from 4 to 5 A. M. Corus,
the name of the north-west wind, here stands for that quarter of
the heavens.

CANTO XII.

First round of the Seventh Circle; those who do violence to others ; Tyrants and Homicides. — The Minotaur. — The Centaurs. — Chiron.— Nessus.— The River of Boiling Blood, and the Sinners in it.

THE place where we came to descend the bank was rugged, and, because of what was there besides, such that every eye would be shy of it.

As is that ruin which, on this side of Trent, struck the Adige on its flank, either by earthquake or by failure of support, — for from the top of the mountain whence it moved, to the plain, the cliff has so fallen down that it might give a path to one who was above, — so was the descent of that ravine. And on the edge of the broken chasm lay stretched out the infamy of Crete, that was conceived in the false cow. And when he saw us he bit himself even as one whom wrath rends inwardly. My Sage cried out toward him, "Perchance thou believest that here is the Duke of Athens who up in the world brought death to thee? Get thee gone, beast, for this one comes not instructed by thy sister, but he goes to behold your punishments."

As a bull that breaks away at the instant he has

now received his mortal stroke, and cannot go, but plunges hither and thither, the Minotaur I saw do the like.

And that wary one cried out, " Run to the pass; while he is raging it is well that thou descend." So we took our way down over the discharge of those stones, which often moved under my feet because of the novel burden.

I was going along thinking, and he said, " Thou thinkest perhaps on this ruin which is guarded by that bestial wrath which I just now quenched. Now would I have thee know that the other time when I descended hither into the nether hell, this cliff had not yet fallen. But in truth, if I discern clearly, a little ere He came, who levied the great spoil on Dis from the supernal circle, in all its parts the deep foul valley trembled so that I thought the universe had felt the love by which, as some believe, oft times the world has been converted into chaos :[1] and, at that moment, this ancient cliff here and elsewhere made this downfall. But fix thine eyes below, for the river of blood is near, in which boils whoso doth harm to others by violence."

[1] Empedocles taught, as Dante may have learned from Aristotle, that Love and Hate were the forces by which the elements of which the world is composed were united and dissociated. The effort of Love was to draw all things into a simple perfect sphere, by which the common order of the world would be brought to chaos.

Oh blind cupidity, both guilty and mad, that so spurs us in the brief life, and then, in the eternal, steeps us so ill!

I saw a broad ditch, bent in an arc, like one that embraces all the plain; according as my Guide had said. And between the foot of the bank and it, in a file were running Centaurs armed with arrows, as they were wont in the world to go to the chase. Seeing us descending, all stopped, and from the troop three detached themselves, with bows and arrows first selected. And one shouted from afar, "To what torment are ye coming, ye who descend the slope? Tell it from there; if not, I draw the bow." My Master said, "We will make answer unto Chiron near you there: ill was it that thy will was ever thus hasty."

Then he touched me, and said, "That is Nessus, who died for the beautiful Dejanira, and he himself wrought vengeance for himself; and that one in the middle, who is gazing on his breast, is the great Chiron who nurtured Achilles. That other is Pholus, who was so full of wrath. Round about the ditch they go by thousands shooting with their arrows what soul lifts itself from the blood more than its guilt has allotted it."

We drew near to those fleet wild beasts. Chiron took a shaft, and with the notch put his beard backward upon his jaw. When he had uncovered

his great mouth he said to his companions, " Are
ye aware that the one behind moves what he
touches? so are not wont to do the feet of the
dead." And my good Leader, who was now at his
breast, where the two natures are conjoined, replied, " Truly he is alive, and thus all alone it behoves me to show him the dark valley: necessity
brings him hither and not delight. One withdrew
from singing alleluiah who committed unto me this
new office ; he is no robber, nor I a thievish spirit.
But, by that power through which I move my steps
along so savage a road, give to us one of thine, to
whom we may be close, that he may show us where
the ford is, and may carry this one on his back, for
he is not a spirit who can go through the air."

Chiron turned upon his right breast, and said to
Nessus, " Turn, and guide them thus, and if another
troop encounter you, make it give way."

We moved on with the trusty escort along the
edge of the crimson boiling, in which the boiled
were making loud shrieks. I saw folk under it up
to the brow, and the great Centaur said, " These
are tyrants who gave themselves to blood and pil-
lage. Here they weep their pitiless offenses: here
is Alexander, and cruel Dionysius who caused Sicily to have woeful years. And that front which
hath such black hair is Azzolino, and that other
who is blond is Opizzo of Esti, who in truth was
slain by his stepson up there in the world."

Then I turned me to the Poet, and he said, " Let him now be first, and I second." A little further on the Centaur stopped above some folk who far as the throat were seen to issue from that boiling stream. He showed to us at one side a solitary shade, and said, " He cleft, in the bosom of God, the heart that still is honored on the Thames." [1] Then I saw folk, who out of the stream held their head, and even all their chest; and of these I recognized many. Thus ever more and more shallow became that blood, until it cooked only the feet: and here was our passage of the foss.

" Even as on this side, thou seest that the boiling stream ever diminishes," said the Centaur, " I would have thee believe that on this other its bed sinks more and more, until it comes round again where it behoves that tyranny should groan. The divine justice here pierces that Attila who was a scourge on earth, and Pyrrhus and Sextus; and forever milks the tears that with the boiling it unlocks from Rinier of Corneto, and from Rinier Pazzo, who upon the highways made such warfare."

Then he turned back and repassed the ford.

[1] In 1271, Prince Henry, son of Richard of Cornwall, was stabbed during the mass, in a church at Viterbo, by Guy of Montfort, to avenge the death of his father, Simon, Earl of Leicester, in 1261. The heart of the young Prince was placed in a golden cup, as Villani (vii. 39) reports, on a column, at the head of a bridge in London.

CANTO XIII.

Second round of the Seventh Circle : of those who have done violence to themselves and to their goods. — The Wood of Self - murderers. — The Harpies. — Pier delle Vigne. — Lano of Siena and others.

NESSUS had not yet reached the yonder bank when we set forward through a wood which was marked by no path. Not green leaves but of a dusky color, not smooth boughs but knotty and gnarled, not fruits were there but thorns with poison. Those savage beasts that hold in hate the tilled places between Cecina and Corneto have no thickets so rough or so dense.

Here the foul Harpies make their nests, who chased the Trojans from the Strophades with dismal announcement of future calamity. They have broad wings, and human necks and faces, feet with claws, and a great feathered belly. They make lament upon the strange trees.

And the good Master, "Before thou enter farther know that thou art in the second round," he began to say to me, "and wilt be, till thou shalt

come unto the horrible sand. Therefore look well
around, and so thou shalt see things that would
take credence from my speech." [1]

I heard wailings uttered on every side, and I saw
no one who might make them, wherefore, I, all
bewildered, stopped.   I believe that he believed
that I believed that all these voices issued amid
those stumps from people who because of us had
hidden themselves.

Therefore said the Master, " If thou break off a
twig from one of these plants, the thoughts thou
hast will all be cut short."   Then I stretched my
hand a little forward and plucked a branchlet from
a great thorn-bush, and its trunk cried out, " Why
dost thou rend me ? "   When it had become dark
with blood it began again to cry, " Why dost thou
tear me? hast thou not any spirit of pity?   Men
we were, and now we are become stocks ; truly
thy hand ought to be more pitiful had we been the
souls of serpents."

As from a green log that is burning at one of its
ends, and from the other drips, and hisses with the
air that is escaping, so from that broken splinter
came out words and blood together ; whereon I let
the tip fall, and stood like a man who is afraid.

" If he had been able to believe before," replied
my Sage, " O wounded soul, what he has seen only

---

[1] Things which if told would seem incredible.

in my verse,[1] he would not upon thee have stretched his hand. But the incredible thing made me prompt him to an act which grieves my very self. But tell him who thou wast, so that, by way of some amends, he may refresh thy fame in the world above, whereto it is allowed him to return."

And the trunk, " So with sweet speech dost thou allure me, that I cannot be silent, and may it not displease you, that I am enticed to speak a little. I am he who held both the keys of the heart of Frederick, and who turned them, locking and unlocking so softly, that from his confidence I kept almost every one.[2] Fidelity so great I bore to the glorious office, that I lost slumber and strength thereby. The harlot,[3] that never from th....erate, Cæsar turned her strumpet eyes, — the co.....on death and vice of courts, — inflamed all min...ds against me, and they, inflamed, did so inflame Au- gustus that my glad honors turned to dismal sor- rows. My mind, in scornful temper thinking to escape scorn by death, made me unjust toward my

[1] In the story of Polydorus, in the third book of the Æneid.

[2] The spirit who speaks is Pier delle Vigne, the Chancellor of Frederick II.; of low birth, he rose to the first place in the state; he was one of the earliest writers of Italian verse. Dante has placed his master as well as him in Hell. See Canto X.

[3] Envie ys lavendere of the court alway ;
For she ne parteth neither nyght ne day
Out of the house of Cesar, thus saith Daunte.
Legende of Goode Women, 358-60.

just self. By the strange roots of this tree I swear
to you, that I never broke faith unto my lord who
was so worthy of honor. And if one of you return eth to the world, let him comfort my memory
that yet lies prostrate from the blow that envy
gave it."

A while he paused, and then, "Since he is
silent," said the Poet to me, "lose not the hour,
but speak and ask of him, if more pleaseth thee."
Whereon I to him, "Do thou ask him further of
what thou thinkest may satisfy me, for I cannot,
such pity fills my heart."

Therefore he began again, "So may this man
do for thee freely what thy speech prays, spirit in-
carcerate, still be pleased to tell us how the soul
is bound within these knots, and tell us, if thou
canst, if any from such limbs is ever loosed."

Then the trunk puffed strongly, and soon that
wind was changed into this voice: "Briefly shall
ye be answered. When the ferocious soul depart-
eth from the body wherefrom itself hath torn itself,
Minos sends it to the seventh gulf. It falls into
the wood, and no part is chosen for it, but where
fortune flings it, there it takes root like a grain of
spelt; it springs up in a shoot and to a wild plant.
The Harpies, feeding then upon its leaves, give
pain, and to the pain a window.[1] Like the rest

[1] The tearing of the leaves gives an outlet to the woe.

we shall go for our spoils,[1] but not, forsooth, that any one may revest himself with them, for it is not just to have that of which one deprives himself. Hither shall we drag them, and through the melancholy wood shall our bodies be suspended, each on the thorn-tree of his molested shade."

We were still attentive to the trunk, believing that it might wish to say more to us, when we were surprised by an uproar, as one who perceives the wild boar and the chase coming toward his stand and hears the beasts and the branches crashing. And behold two on the left hand, naked and scratched, flying so violently that they broke all the limbs of the wood. The one in front was shouting, " Now, help, help, Death ! " and the other, who seemed to himself too slow, " Lano, thy legs were not so nimble at the jousts of the Toppo: " [2] and when perhaps his breath was failing, of himself and of a bush he made a group. Behind them the wood was full of black bitches, ravenous and running like greyhounds that have been unleashed. On him that had squatted they set their teeth and tore him to pieces, bit by bit, then carried off his woeful limbs.

---

[1] Our bodies, at the Last Judgment.

[2] Lano was slain in flight at the defeat of the Sienese by the Aretines, near the Pieve del Toppo, in 1280. He and Jacomo were notorious prodigals.

My Guide then took me by the hand, and led me to the bush, which was weeping through its bleeding breaks in vain. " O Jacomo of Sant' Andrea," it was saying, " what hath it vantaged thee to make of me a screen? What blame have I for thy wicked life?" When the Master had stopped beside it, he said, " Who wast thou, who through so many wounds blowest forth with blood thy woeful speech?" And he to us, " O souls who art arrived to see the shameful ravage that hath thus disjoined my leaves from me, collect them at the foot of the wretched bush. I was of the city which for the Baptist changed her first patron;[1] wherefore will he always make her sorrowful with his art. And were it not that at the passage of the Arno some semblance of him yet remains, those citizens who afterwards rebuilt it upon the ashes that were left by Attila[2] would have labored in vain. I made a gibbet for myself of my own dwelling."

[1] The first patron of Florence was Mars ; a fragment of a statue of whom stood till 1333 on the Ponte Vecchio.

[2] It was not Attila, but Totila, who in 542 besieged Florence, and, according to false popular tradition, burned it. The names and personages were frequently confounded in the Dark Ages.

CANTO XIV.

Third round of the Seventh Circle : of those who have done violence to God. — The Burning Sand. — Capaneus. — Figure of the Old Man in Crete. — The Rivers of Hell.

BECAUSE the charity of my native place constrained me, I gathered up the scattered leaves and gave them back to him who was already hoarse.

Then we came to the confine, where the second round is divided from the third, and where is seen a horrible mode of justice.

To make clearly manifest the new things, I say that we had reached a plain which from its bed removeth every plant. The woeful wood is a garland round about it, even as the dismal foss to that. Here, on the very edge, we stayed our steps. The floor was a dry and dense sand, not made in other fashion than that which of old was trodden by the feet of Cato.

O vengeance of God, how much thou oughtest to be feared by every one who readeth that which was manifest unto mine eyes !

Of naked souls I saw many flocks, that were all weeping very miserably, and diverse law seemed imposed upon them. Some folk were lying supine on the ground, some were seated all crouched up, and others were going about continually. Those who were going around were far the more, and those the fewer who were lying down under the torment, but they had their tongues more loose for wailing.

Over all the sand, with a slow falling, were raining down dilated flakes of fire, as of snow on alps without a wind. As the flames which Alexander in those hot parts of India saw falling upon his host, solid to the ground, wherefore he took care to trample the soil by his troops, because the vapor was better extinguished while it was single; so was descending the eternal glow whereby the sand was kindled, like tinder beneath the steel, for doubling of the dole. Without repose was ever the dance of the wretched hands, now there, now here, brushing from them the fresh burning.

I began, "Master, thou that overcomest everything, except the obdurate demons, who at the entrance of the gate came out against us, who is that great one that seemeth not to heed the fire, and lies scornful and contorted, so that the rain seems not to ripen him?" And that same one who had perceived that I was asking my Leader about him, cried out, "Such as I was alive, such am I dead. Though Jove weary his smith, from whom in wrath he took the sharp thunderbolt wherewith on my last day I was smitten, or though he weary the others, turn by turn, in Mongibello at the black forge, crying, ' Good Vulcan, help, help! ' even as he did at the fight of Phlegra, and should hurl on me with all his might, thereby he should not have glad vengeance."

Then my Leader spoke ·with force so great that I had not heard him so loud, " O Capaneus, in that thy pride is not quenched, art thou the more punished ; no torture save thine own rage would be a pain adequate to thy fury."

Then he turned round to me with better look, saying, " He was one of the Seven Kings that besieged Thebes, and he held, and it appears that he holds God in disdain, and little it appears that he prizes Him ; but as I said to him, his own despites are very due adornments for his breast. Now come on behind me, and take heed withal, not to set thy feet upon the burning sand, but keep them always close unto the wood."

Silent we came to where spirts forth from the wood a little streamlet, the redness of which still makes me shudder. As from the Bulicame issues a brooklet, which then the sinful women share among them, so this down across the sand went along.[1] Its bed and both its sloping banks were

---

[1] The Bulicame, a hot spring near Viterbo, much frequented

made of stone, and the margins on the side, whereby I perceived that the crossing [1] was there.

"Among all else that I have shown to thee,
since we entered through the gate whose threshold
is barred to no one, nothing has been discerned by
thine eyes so notable as is the present stream
which deadens all the flamelets upon it." These
words were of my Leader, wherefore I prayed him,
that he should give me largess of the food for
which he had given me largess of desire.

"In mid sea sits a wasted land," said he then,
"which is named Crete, under whose king the
world of old was chaste. A mountain is there that
of old was glad with waters and with leaves, which
is called Ida; now it is desert, like a thing out-
worn. Rhea chose it of old for the trusty cradle
of her little son, and to conceal him better when
he cried had shoutings made there. Within the
mountain stands erect a great old man, who holds
his shoulders turned towards Damietta, and looks
at Rome as if his mirror. His head is formed of
fine gold, and pure silver are his arms and breast;
then he is of brass far as to the fork. From there
downward he is all of chosen iron, save that his
right foot is of baked clay, and he stands erect on

as a bath, the use of a portion of which was assigned to "sinful
women."

[1] The crossing of the breadth of the round of burning sand, on
the way inward toward the next circle.

that more than on the other.[1] Every part except
the gold is cleft with a fissure that trickles tears,
which collected perforate that cavern. Their course
falls from rock to rock into this valley ; they form
Acheron, Styx, and Phlegethon ; then it goes down
through this narrow channel far as where there is
no more descending. They form Cocytus, and
what that pool is, thou shalt see ; therefore here is
it not told."

And I to him, " If the present rill floweth down
thus from our world, why doth it appear to us only
at this rim ? "

And he to me, " Thou knowest that the place is
round, and though thou art come far, ever to the
left descending toward the bottom, not yet hast
thou turned through the whole circle ; wherefore
if a new thing appears to us, it ought not to bring
wonder to thy face."

And I again, " Master, where are Phlegethon
and Lethe found, for of the one thou art silent,
and of the other thou sayest that it is formed by
this rain ? "

" In all thy questions surely thou pleasest me,"

---

[1] This image is taken directly from the dream of Nebuchad-
nezzar (Daniel ii. 31–33). It is the type of the ages of tradition
and history, with its back to the past, its face toward Rome,—the
seat of the Empire and of the Church. The tears of the sin and
suffering of the generations of man form the rivers of Hell.

he answered, " but the boiling of the red water ought truly to solve one that thou askest. Lethe thou shalt see, but outside of this ditch, there where souls go to lave themselves when sin repented of is taken away." Then he said, " Now it is time to depart from the wood ; take heed that thou come behind me ; the margins afford way, for they are not burning, and above them all the vapor is extinguished."

CANTO XV.

Third round of the Seventh Circle : of those who have done violence to Nature. — Brunetto Latini. — Prophecies of misfortune to Dante.

Now one of the hard margins bears us on, and the fume of the brook overshadows so that it saves the water and the banks from the fire. As the Flemings, between Wissant and Bruges, fearing the flood that is blown in upon them, make the dyke whereby the sea is routed; and as the Paduans along the Brenta, in order to defend their towns and castles, ere Chiarentana [1] feel the heat, — in such like were these made, though neither so high nor so thick had the master, whoever he was, made them.

We were now so remote from the wood that I could not have seen where it was though I had turned me round to look, when we encountered a troop of souls which was coming along by the bank, and each of them was looking at us, as at eve one is wont to look at another under the new

---

[1] The mountain range north of the Brenta, by the floods from which the river is swollen in the spring.

moon, and they so sharpened their brows toward
us as the old tailor does on the needle's eye.

Thus gazed at by that company, I was recognized by one who took me by the hem, and cried
out, "What a marvel!" And when he stretched
out his arm to me, I fixed my eyes on his baked
aspect so that his scorched visage prevented not
my mind from recognizing him; and bending down
my own to his face, I answered, "Are you here,
Sir Brunetto?"[1] And he, "O my son, let it not
displease thee if Brunetto Latini turn a little back
with thee, and let the train go on." I said to him,
"With all my power I pray this of you, and if you
will that I seat myself with you I will do so, if it
pleaseth this one, for I go with him." "O son,"
said he, "whoever of this herd stops for an instant
lies then a hundred years without fanning himself
when the fire smites him; therefore go onward, I
will come at thy skirts, and then I will rejoin my
band which goeth weeping its eternal sufferings."

---

[1] Brunetto Latini, one of the most learned and able Florentines
of the thirteenth century. He was banished with the other chiefs
of the Guelph party, after the battle of Montaperti, in 1260, and
went to France, where he resided for many years. After his return to Florence he became Secretary of the Commune, and he
was the master of Dante and Guido Cavalcanti. His principal
literary work was *Li Livres dou Tresor*, written in French, an
interesting compend of the *omne scibile*. He died in 1290. Dante
uses the plural " you " in addressing him, as a sign of respect.

I dared not descend from the road to go level with him, but I held my head bowed like one who goes reverently. He began, " What fortune, or destiny, ere the last day, brings thee down here? and who is this that shows the road?"

" There above, in the clear life," I answered him, " I lost myself in a valley, before my time was full. Only yester morn I turned my back on it; this one [1] appeared to me as I was returning to it, and he is leading me homeward along this path."

And he to me: " If thou follow thy star, thou canst not miss the glorious port, if, in the beautiful life, I discerned aright. And if I had not so untimely died, seeing heaven so benignant unto thee I would have given cheer unto thy work. But that ungrateful populace malign which descended from Fiesole of old,[2] and smacks yet of the mountain and the rock, will hate thee because of thy good deeds; and this is right, for among the bitter sorb-

[1] Dante never speaks Virgil's name in Hell.

[2] After his flight from Rome Catiline betook himself to Faesulae (Fiesole), and here for a time held out against the Roman forces. The popular tradition ran that, after his defeat, Faesulae was destroyed, and its people, together with a colony from Rome, made a settlement on the banks of the Arno, below the mountain on which Faesulae had stood. The new town was named Fiora, *siccome fosse in fiora edificata*, " as though built among flowers," but afterwards was called Fiorenza, or Florence. See G. Villani, *Cronica*, I. xxxi.-xxxviii.

trees it is not fitting the sweet fig should bear
fruit. Old report in the world calls them blind ;
it is a people avaricious, envious, and proud ; from
their customs take heed that thou keep thyself
clean. Thy fortune reserves such honor for thee
that one party and the other shall hunger for thee ;
but far from the goat shall be the grass. Let the
Fiesolan beasts make litter of themselves, and
touch not the plant, if any spring still upon their
dungheap, in which may live again the holy seed
of those Romans who remained there when it became the nest of so much malice."

"If all my entreaty were fulfilled," replied I to
him, "you would not yet be placed in banishment
from human nature ; for in my mind is fixed, and
now fills my heart, the dear, good, paternal image
of you, when in the world hour by hour you taught
me how man makes himself eternal · and in what
gratitude I hold it, so long as I live, it behoves
that on my tongue should be discerned. That
which you tell me of my course I write, and re-
serve it to be glossed with other text,[1] by a Lady,
who will know how, if I attain to her. Thus much
would I have manifest to you: if only that my conscience chide me not, for Fortune, as she will, I am

---

[1] The prophecy by Ciacco of the fall of Dante's party, Canto
vi., and that by Farinata of Dante's exile, Canto x., which Virgil
had told should be made clear to him by Beatrice.

ready. Such earnest is not strange unto my ears; therefore let Fortune turn her wheel as pleases her, and the churl his mattock."[1]

My Master then upon his right side turned himself back, and looked at me; then said, "He listens well who notes it."

Not the less for this do I go on speaking with Sir Brunetto, and I ask, who are his most known and most eminent companions. And he to me, "To know of some is good, of the others silence will be laudable for us, for the time would be short for so much speech. In brief, know that all were clerks, and great men of letters, and of great fame, defiled in the world with one same sin. Priscian goes along with that disconsolate crowd, and Francesco of Accorso;[2] and thou mightest also have seen, hadst thou had desire of such scurf, him who by the Servant of Servants was translated from Arno to Bacchiglione, where he left his ill-strained nerves.[3] Of more would I tell, but the going on and the speech cannot be longer, for I see yonder a new cloud rising from the sand. Folk come with

[1] The churl of Fiesole.

[2] Priscian, the famous grammarian of the sixth century; Francis of Accorso, a jurist of great repute, who taught at Oxford and at Bologna, and died in 1294.

[3] Andrea de' Mozzi, bishop of Florence, translated by Boniface VIII. to Vicenza, near which the Bacchiglione runs. He died in 1296.

whom I must not be. Let my Tesoro be commended to thee, in which I still am living, and
more I ask not."

Then he turned back, and seemed of those who
run at Verona for the green cloth [1] across the plain,
and of these he seemed the one that wins, and not
he that loses.

[1] The prize in the annual races at Verona.

CANTO XVI.

Third round of the Seventh Circle : of those who have done violence to Nature. — Guido Guerra, Tegghiaio Aldobrandi and Jacopo Rusticucci. — The roar of Phlegethon as it pours downward. — The cord thrown into the abyss.

Now was I in a place where the resounding of the water that was falling into the next circle was heard, like that hum which the beehives make, when three shades together separated themselves, running, from a troop that was passing under the rain of the bitter torment. They came toward us, and each cried out, "Stop thou, that by thy garb seemest to us to be one from our wicked city!"

Ah me! what wounds I saw upon their limbs, recent and old, burnt in by the flames. Still it grieves me for them but to remember it.

To their cries my Teacher gave heed ; he turned his face toward me, and "Now wait," he said ; "to these one should be courteous, and were it not for the fire that the nature of the place shoots out, I should say that haste better befitted thee than them."

They began again, when we stopped, the old

verse, and when they had reached us they made
a wheel of themselves all three. As champions
naked and oiled are wont to do, watching their
hold and their vantage, before they come to blows
and thrusts, thus, wheeling, each directed his face
on me, so that his neck in contrary direction to his
feet was making continuous journey.

"Ah ! if the misery of this shifting sand bring
us and our prayers into contempt," began one,
"and our darkened and blistered aspect, let our
fame incline thy mind to tell us who thou art, that
so securely plantest thy living feet in Hell. He
whose tracks thou seest me trample, though he go
naked and singed, was of greater state than thou
thinkest. Grandson he was of the good Gual-
drada; his name was Guidoguerra, and in his life
he did much with counsel, and with the sword.
The other who treads the sand behind me is Tegghiaio Aldobrandi, whose fame should be welcome
in the world above. And I, who am set with them
on the cross, was Jacopo Rusticucci,[1] and surely
my savage wife more than aught else injures me."

---

[1] Concerning Tegghiaio and Rusticucci Dante had enquired of
Ciacco, Canto vi. They and Guido Guerra were illustrious citizens of Florence in the thirteenth century. Their deeds are recorded by Villani and Ricordano Malespini. The good Gual-
drada, famed for her beauty and her modesty, was the daughter
of Messer Bellincione Berti, referred to in Cantos xv. and xvi. of
Paradise as one of the early worthies of the city. See G. Villani, *Cronica.* V. xxxvii.

If I could have been sheltered from the fire I would have cast myself below among them, and I think that the Teacher would have permitted it; but because I should have been scorched and baked, fear overcame my good will that made me greedy to embrace them. Then I began: "Not contempt, but grief, did your condition fix within me, so that slowly will it be all divested, soon as this my Lord said words to me by which I understood that such folk as ye are might be coming. Of your city I am; and always your deeds and honored names have I retraced and heard with affection. I leave the gall and go for the sweet fruits promised me by my veracious Leader; but far as the centre needs must I first descend."

"So may thy soul long direct thy limbs," replied he then, "and so may thy fame shine after thee, say if courtesy and valor abide in our city as they were wont, or if they have quite gone forth from it? For Guglielmo Borsiere,[1] who is in torment with us but short while, and goes yonder with our companions, afflicts us greatly with his words."

"The new people and the sudden gains[2] have generated pride and excess, Florence, in thee, so

---

[1] Nothing is known from contemporary record of Borsiere, but Boccaccio tells a story of him in the *Decameron*, giorn. i. nov. 8.

[2] Florence had grown rapidly in population and in wealth during the last years of the thirteenth century.

that already thou weepest thereat." Thus cried I
with face uplifted. And the three, who understood
that for answer, looked one at the other, as men
look at hearing truth.

" If other times it costeth thee so little," replied
they all, "to satisfy others, happy thou that thus
speakest at thy pleasure. Therefore, if thou es-
capest from these dark places, and returnest to
see again the beautiful stars, when it shall rejoice
thee to say, ' I have been,' mind thou speak of
us unto the people." Then they broke the wheel,
and in flying their swift legs seemed wings.

Not an amen could have been said so quickly as
they had disappeared; wherefore it seemed good
to my Master to depart. I followed him, and we
had gone little way before the sound of the water
was so near to us, that had we spoken we scarce
had heard. As that river on the left slope of
the Apennine, which, the first from Monte Veso
toward the east, has its proper course, — which is
called Acquacheta up above, before it sinks valleyward into its low bed, and at Forlì no longer has
that name,[1] — reverberates from the alp in falling
with a single leap there above San Benedetto,

---

[1] At Forlì the river is called the Montone; it was the first of
the rivers on the left of the Apennines that had its course to the
sea; the others before it being tributaries of the Po, which rises
on Monte Veso.

where there ought to be shelter for a thousand;[1] thus down from a precipitous bank we found that dark-tinted water resounding, so that in short while it would have hurt the ears.

I had a cord girt around me, and with it I had once thought to take the leopard of the dappled skin.[2] After I had loosed it wholly from me, even as my Leader had commanded me, I reached it to him wound up and coiled. Whereon he turned toward the right, and somewhat far from the edge threw it down.into that deep abyss. "And surely some strange thing must needs respond," said I to myself, "to the strange signal which the Master so follows with his eye."

Ah! how cautious men ought to be near those who see not only the act, but with their wisdom look within the thoughts. He said to me: "Soon will come up that which I await, and what thy thought is dreaming must soon discover itself unto thy sight."

To that truth which has the aspect of falsehood ought one always to close his lips so far as he can,

[1] These last words are obscure, and none of the commentators explain them satisfactorily.

[2] The leopard of the dappled skin, which had often turned back Dante from the Mountain to the Dark Wood (see Canto i.); the type of sensual sin. The cord is the type of religious asceticism, of which the poet no longer has need. The meaning of its use as a signal is not apparent.

because without fault it causes shame;[1] but here I cannot be silent, and by the notes of this comedy, Reader, I swear to thee, — so may they not be void of lasting grace, — that I saw through that thick and dark air a shape come swimming upwards marvelous to every steadfast heart; like as he returns who goes down sometimes to loose an anchor that grapples either a rock or other thing that in the sea is hid, who stretches upward, and draws in his feet.

---

[1] Because the narrator is falsely taxed with falsehood.

CANTO XVII.

Third round of the Seventh Circle : of those who have done violence to Art. — Geryon. — The Usurers. — Descent to the Eighth Circle.

" BEHOLD the wild beast with the pointed tail, that passes mountains, and breaks walls and weapons; behold him that infects all the world."[1] Thus began my Leader to speak to me; and he beckoned to him that he should come to shore near the end of the trodden marbles.[2] And that loathsome image of fraud came onward, and landed his head and his body, but drew not his tail upon the bank. His face was the face of a just man (so benignant was its skin outwardly), and of a serpent all the trunk beside; he had two paws, hairy to the armpits; his back and breast and both his sides were painted with nooses and circles. With more colors of woof and warp Tartars or

---

[1] Dante makes Geryon the type and image of Fraud, thus allegorizing the triple form (*forma tricorporis umbrae : Aeneid* vi. 289; *tergemini Geryonae ; Id.* viii. 292) ascribed to him by the ancient poets.

[2] The stony margin of Phlegethon, on which Virgil and Dante have crossed the sand.

Turks never made cloth, nor were such webs woven by Arachne.

As sometimes boats lie on the shore, so that they are partly in water and partly on the ground, and as yonder, among the gluttonous Germans, the beaver settles himself to make his war,[1] so lay that worst of beasts upon the rim that closes in the sand with stone. In the void all his tail was quivering, twisting upwards its venomous fork, which like a scorpion's armed the point.

The Leader said: "Now needs must our way bend a little toward that wicked beast that is couching there." Therefore we descended on the right hand and took ten steps upon the verge quite to avoid the sand and flame. And when we had come to it, I see, a little farther on, people sitting upon the sand near to the void place.[2]

Here the Master said to me: "In order that thou mayst bear away complete experience of this round, now go and see their condition. Let thy discourse there be brief. Till thou returnest I will speak with this one, that he may concede to us his strong shoulders."

---

[1] With his tail in the water to catch his prey, as was popularly believed.

[2] These people are the third class of sinners punished in this round of the Seventh Circle, those who have done violence to Art, the usurers. (See Canto xi.)

Thus, still up by the extreme head of that seventh circle, all alone, I went where the sad people were sitting. Through the eyes their woe was bursting forth. This way and that they helped with their hands, sometimes against the vapors,[1] and sometimes against the hot soil. Not otherwise do the dogs in summer, now with muzzle, now with paw, when they are bitten either by fleas, or flies, or gadflies. When I set my eyes on the face of some on whom the woeful fire falls, not one of them I recognized;[2] but I perceived that from the neck of each was hanging a pouch, that had a certain color and a certain device,[3] and thereupon it seems their eyes feed. And as I looking come among them, I saw upon a yellow purse azure that had the face and bearing of a lion.[4] Then as the current of my look proceeded I saw another, red as blood, display a goose whiter than butter. And one, who had his little white bag marked with an azure and pregnant sow,[5] said to me, " What art thou doing in this ditch? Now get thee gone, and

---

[1] The falling flames.

[2] Dante thus indicates that they were not worthy to be known.

[3] The blazon of their arms, by which Dante learns who they are.

[4] This was the device of the Gianfigliazzi, a Guelph family of Florence ; the next was that of the Ubriachi, Ghibellines, also of Florence.

[5] Arms of the Scrovigni of Padua.

since thou art still alive, know that my neighbor,
Vitaliano, will sit here at my left side. With these
Florentines am I, a Paduan; often they stun my
ears shouting, 'Let the sovereign cavalier come
who will bring the pouch with the three goats.'"[1]
Then he twisted his mouth, and stuck out his
tongue, like an ox that licks his nose.

And I, fearing lest longer stay might vex him
who had admonished me to stay but little, turned
back from these weary souls. I found my Leader,
who had already mounted upon the croup of the
fierce animal, and he said to me, "Now be strong
and courageous; henceforth the descent is by such
stairs;[2] mount thou in front, for I wish to be between, so that the tail cannot do thee harm."

As is he who hath the shivering fit of the quar-
tan so near that his nails are already pallid, and he
is all of a tremble only looking at the shade, such I
became at these words uttered. But his reproaches
wrought shame in me, which in presence of a good
lord makes a servant strong.

I seated myself on those huge shoulders. I
wished to speak thus, "Take heed that thou embrace me," but the voice came not as I had thought.

[1] One Giovanni Buiamonte of Florence, "who surpassed all
others of the time in usury," says Benvenuto da Imola.

[2] Not by foot, nor by boat as heretofore, but carried by living
ministers of Hell.

But he who other time had succored me, in other
peril, soon as I mounted, clasped and sustained
me with his arms: and he said, " Geryon, move
on now; let the circles be wide, and the descending slow; consider the strange burden that thou
hast."

As a little vessel goeth from its place, backward,
backward, so he thence withdrew; and when he
felt himself quite at play, he turned his tail to
where his breast had been, and moved it, stretched
out like an eel, and with his paws gathered the air
to himself. Greater fear I do not think there was
when Phaëthon abandoned the reins, whereby heaven,
as is still apparent, was scorched; nor when the
wretched Icarus felt his flanks unfeathering through
the melting of the wax, his father shouting to him,
"Ill way thou holdest," than mine was, when I
saw that I was in the air on every side, and saw
every sight vanished, except that of the beast. He
goes along swimming very slowly, wheels and descends, but I perceive it not, save by the wind upon
my face, and from below.

I heard now on the right hand the gorge making
beneath us a horrible roar; wherefore I stretch
out my head, with my eyes downward. Then I became more afraid to lean over, because I saw fires
and heard laments; whereat I, trembling, wholly
cowered back. And I saw then, what I had not

seen before, the descending and the wheeling, by the great evils that were drawing near on diverse sides.

As the falcon which has been long on wing, that, without sight of lure or bird, makes the falconer say, " Ah me, thou stoopest ! " — descends weary, there whence he had set forth swiftly, through a hundred circles, and lights far from his master, disdainful and sullen ; so Geryon set us at the bottom, at the very foot of the scarped rock, and, disburdened of our persons, darted away as arrow from the bowstring.

CANTO XVIII.

Eighth Circle: the first pit: 'panders and seducers. —
Venedico Caccianimico. — Jason. — Second pit: false flat-
terers. — Alessio Interminei. — Thais.

THERE is a place in Hell called Malebolge, all
of stone of the color of iron, as is the encircling
wall that surrounds it. Right in the middle of
this field malign yawns an abyss exceeding wide
and deep, the structure of which I will tell of in its
place. That belt, therefore, which remains between
the abyss and the foot of the high bank is circular, and it has its ground divided into ten valleys.
Such an aspect as where, for guard of the walls,
many moats encircle castles, the place where they
are presents, such image did these make here. And
as in such strongholds from their thresholds to the
outer bank are little bridges, so from the base of
the precipitous wall started crags which traversed
the dykes and the moats far as the abyss that collects and cuts them off.

In this place, shaken off from the back of Geryon, we found ourselves; and the Poet held to
the left, and I moved on behind. On the right

hand I saw new sorrow, new torments, and new scourgers, with which the first pit[1] was replete. At its bottom were the sinners naked. This side the middle they came facing us; on the farther side with us, but with swifter pace. As the Romans, because of the great host in the year of Jubilee,[2] have taken means upon the bridge for the passage of the people, who on one side all have their front toward the Castle,[3] and go to Saint Peter's, and on the other toward the Mount.[4]

Along the gloomy rock, on this side and on that, I saw horned demons with great scourges, who were beating them cruelly from behind. Ah! how they made them lift their heels at the first blows; truly not one waited for the second, or the third.

While I was going on, my eyes encountered one, and I said straightway, "Ere now for sight of him I have not fasted;" wherefore to shape him out I stayed my feet, and the sweet Leader stopped with me, and assented to my going somewhat back. And that scourged one thought to conceal himself by lowering his face, but little it availed him, for I said: "O thou that castest thine eye upon the ground, if the features that thou bearest are not

---

[1] *Bolgia*, literally, budget, purse, sack, here used for circular valley, or pit.

[2] The year 1299–1300, from Christmas to Easter.

[3] Of Sant' Angelo.   [4] The Capitoline.

false, thou art Venedico Caccianimico; but what brings thee unto such pungent sauces?"

And he to me, "Unwillingly I tell it, but thy clear speech compels me, which makes me recollect the olden world. I was he who brought the beautiful Ghisola[1] to do the will of the Marquis, however the shameful tale may be reported. And not the only Bolognese do I weep here, nay, this place is so full of them, that so many tongues are not now taught between Savena and the Reno to say *sipa;*[2] and if of this thou wishest pledge or testimony, bring to mind our avaricious heart." As he spoke thus a demon struck him with his scourge and said, "Begone, pandar, here are no women for coining."

I rejoined my Escort; then with few steps we came to where a crag jutted from the bank.[3] Easily enough we ascended it, and turning to the right[4] upon its ridge, from those eternal circles we departed.

---

[1] His own sister; the unseemly tale is known only through Dante and his fourteenth-century commentators, and the latter, while agreeing that the Marquis was one of the Esti of Ferrara, do not agree as to which of them he was.

[2] Bologna lies between the Savena and the Reno; *sipa* is the Bolognese form of *sia*, or *si*.

[3] Forming a bridge, thrown like an arch across the pit.

[4] The course of the Poets, which has mostly been to the left through the upper Circles, is now generally to proceed straight

When we were there where it opens below to give passage to the scourged, the Leader said, "Stop, and let the sight strike on thee of these other miscreants, of whom thou hast not yet seen the face, because they have gone along in the same direction with us."

From the ancient bridge we looked at the train that was coming toward us from the other side, and which the whip in like manner drives on. The good Master, without my asking, said to me, " Look at that great one who is coming, and seems not to shed a tear for pain. What royal aspect he still retains ! He is Jason, who by courage and by wit despoiled the Colchians of their ram. He passed by the isle of Lemnos, after the undaunted women pitiless had given all their males to death. There with tokens and with ornate words he deceived Hypsipyle, the maiden, who first had deceived all the rest. There he left her pregnant, and alone; such sin condemns him to such torment; and also for Medea is vengeance done. With him goes whoso in such wise deceives. And let this suffice to know of the first valley, and of those that it holds in its fangs."

across the lower Circles where Fraud is punished. They had been going to the left at the foot of the precipice, and consequently turn to the right to ascend the bridge. The allegorical intention in the direction of their course is evident.

Now we were where the narrow path sets across the second dyke, and makes of it shoulders for another arch. Here we heard people moaning in the next pit, and snorting with their muzzles, and with their palms beating themselves. The banks were encrusted with a mould because of the breath from below that sticks on them, and was making quarrel with the eyes and with the nose. The bottom is so hollowed out that no place sufficeth us for seeing it, without mounting on the crest of the arch where the crag rises highest. Hither we came, and thence, down in the ditch, I saw people plunged in an excrement that seemed as if it proceeded from human privies.

And while I am searching down there with my eye, I saw one with his head so foul with ordure that it was not apparent whether he were layman or clerk. He shouted to me, " Why art so greedy to look more at me than at the other filthy ones ? " And I to him, " Because, if I remember rightly, ere now I have seen thee with dry hair, and thou art Alessio Interminei of Lucca [1] ; therefore I eye thee more than all the rest." And he then, beating his pate, " Down here those flatteries wherewith my tongue was never cloyed have submerged me."

Hereupon my Leader, " Mind thou push thy sight a little farther forward so that with thine eyes thou

[1] Of him nothing is known but what these words tell.

mayest quite reach the face of that dirty and dis-
heveled creature, who is scratching herself there
with her nasty nails, and now is crouching down and
now standing on foot. She is Thais the prostitute,
who answered her paramour when he said, ' Have I
great thanks from thee?' — 'Nay, marvelous.' " [1]
And herewith let our sight be satisfied.

[1] These words are derived from Terence, *Eunuchus*, act iii.
sc. 1.

CANTO XIX.

Eighth Circle : third pit : simonists. — Pope Nicholas III.

OH Simon Magus! Oh ye his wretched follow-ers, who, rapacious, do prostitute for gold and silver the things of God that ought to be the brides of righteousness, now it behoves for you the trumpet sound, since ye are in the third pit!

Already were we come to the next tomb,[1] mounted on that part of the crag which just above the middle of the ditch hangs plumb. Oh Supreme Wisdom, how great is the art that Thou displayest in Heaven, on Earth, and in the Evil World! and how justly doth Thy Power distribute!

I saw along the sides, and over the bottom, the livid stone full of holes all of one size, and each was circular. They seemed to me not less wide nor larger than those that in my beautiful Saint John are made as place for the baptizers;[2] one of

---

[1] The next *bolgia* or pit.

[2] "My beautiful Saint John" is the Baptistery at Florence. In Dante's time the infants, born during the year, were all here bap-tized by immersion, mostly on the day of St. John Baptist, the 24th of June. There was a large circular font in the middle of

which, not many years ago, I broke for sake of one
who was stifling in it; and be this the seal to un-
deceive all men. Forth from the mouth of each
protruded the feet of a sinner, and his legs up to
the calf, and the rest was within. The soles of all
were both on fire, wherefore their joints quivered
so violently that they would have snapped withes
and bands. As the flaming of things oiled is wont
to move only on the outer surface, so was it there
from the heels to the toes.

"Who is he, Master, that writhes, quivering
more than the others his consorts," said I, "and
whom a ruddier flame is sucking?" And he to
me, "If thou wilt that I carry thee down there by
that bank which slopes the most,[1] from him thou
shalt know of himself and of his wrongs." And
I, "Whatever pleaseth thee even so is good to me.
Thou art Lord, and knowest that I part me not
from thy will, and thou knowest that which is un-
spoken."

Then we went upon the fourth dyke, turned, and
descended on the left hand, down to the bottom
pierced with holes, and narrow. And the good

the church, and around it in its marble wall were four cylindrical
standing-places for the priests, closed by doors, to protect them
from the pressure of the crowd.

[1] The whole of·the Eighth circle slopes toward the centre, so
that the inner wall of each *bolgia* is lower, and is less sharply inclined than the outer.

Master set me not down yet from his haunch, till he brought me to the cleft of him who was thus lamenting with his shanks.

"O whoe'er thou art, that keepest upside down, sad soul, planted like a stake," I began to say, "speak, if thou canst." I was standing like the friar who confesses the perfidious assassin,[1] who, after he is fixed, recalls him, in order to delay his death.

And he[2] cried out, "Art thou already standing there? Art thou already standing there, Boniface? By several years the record lied to me. Art thou so quickly sated with that having, for which thou didst not fear to seize by guile the beautiful Lady,[3] and then to do her outrage?"

Such I became as those that, not comprehending that which is replied to them, stand as if mocked, and know not what to answer.

Then Virgil said, "Tell him quickly, I am not he, I am not he thou thinkest." And I answered as was enjoined on me; whereat the spirit quite twisted

---

[1] Such criminals were not infrequently punished by being set, head downwards, in a hole in which they were buried alive.

[2] This is Nicholas III., pope from 1277 to 1280; he takes Dante to be Boniface VIII., but Boniface was not to die till 1303. Compare what Nicholas says of "the record" with Farinata's statement, in Canto X, concerning the foresight of the damned.

[3] The Church, to which Boniface did outrage in many forms; but worst by his simoniacal practices.

his feet. Thereafter, sighing and with tearful voice, he said to me, " Then what dost thou require of me? If to know who I am concerneth thee so much that thou hast crossed the bank therefor, know that I was vested with the Great Mantle ; and verily I was a son of the She-Bear,[1] so eager to advance the cubs, that up there I put wealth, and here myself, into the purse. Beneath my head are stretched the others that preceded me in simony, flattened through the fissures of the rock. There below shall I likewise sink, when he shall come whom I believed thou wert, then when I put to thee the sudden question ; but already the time is longer that I have cooked my feet, and that I have been thus upside down, than he will stay planted with red feet ; for after him will come, of uglier deed, from westward, a shepherd without law,[2] such as must cover him and me again. A new Jason will he be, of whom it is read in Maccabees ;[3] and as to that one his king was compliant, so unto this he who rules France shall be." [4]

[1] Nicholas was of the *Orsini* family.

[2] Clement V., who will come from Avignon, and in a little more than ten years after the death of Boniface. Nicholas had already " cooked his feet " for twenty years. The prophecy of the death of Clement after a shorter time affords an indication that this canto was not written until after 1314, the year of his death.

[3] The story of Jason, " that ungodly wretch and no high-priest " who bought the high-priesthood from King Antiochus, is told in 2 Maccabees iv. Its application to the Pope was plain.

[4] "He who rules France " was Philip the Fair.

I know not if here I was too audacious that I
only answered him in this strain, " Pray now tell
me how much treasure our Lord desired of Saint
Peter before he placed the keys in his keeping?
Surely he required nothing save ' Follow me.'
Nor did Peter or the others require of Matthias
gold or silver, when he was chosen to the place
which the guilty soul had lost. Therefore stay thou,
for thou art rightly punished, and guard well the
ill-gotten money that against Charles [1] made thee to
be bold. And were it not that reverence for the
Supreme Keys that thou heldest in the glad life
still forbiddeth me, I would use words still more
grave ; for your avarice saddens the world, tram-
pling down the good and exalting the bad. Of you
shepherds the Evangelist was aware, when she that
sitteth upon the waters was seen by him to forni-
cate with kings : that woman that was born with
the seven heads, and from the ten horns had evi-
dence, so long as virtue pleased her spouse.[2] Ye
have made you a god of gold and silver : and what

[1] Charles of Anjou, of whom Nicholas III. was the enemy.
He was charged with having been bribed to support the attempt
to expel the French from Sicily, which began with the Sicilian
Vespers in 1282.

[2] Dante deals freely with the figures of the Apocalypse : Revelation xvii. The woman here stands for the Church ; her seven
heads may be interpreted as the Seven Sacraments, and her ten
horns as the Commandments ; her spouse is the Pope.

difference is there between you and the idolater
save that he worships one and ye a hundred? Ah
Constantine! of how much ill was mother, not thy
conversion, but that dowry which the first rich
Father received from thee!"[1]

And, while I was singing these notes to him,
whether anger or conscience stung him, he violently quivered with both feet. I believe, forsooth,
that it had pleased my Leader, with so contented
look he listened ever to the sound of the true words
uttered. Thereupon with both his arms he took
me, and when he had me wholly on his breast, remounted on the way by which he had descended.
Nor did he tire of holding me clasped till he had
borne me up to the summit of the arch which is
the passage from the fourth to the fifth dyke.
Here softly he laid down his burden, softly because of the ragged and steep crag, that would be
a difficult pass for goats. Thence another great
valley was discovered to me.

[1] The reference is to the so-called Donation of Constantine, the
reality of which was generally accepted till long after Dante's
time.

CANTO XX.

Eighth Circle : fourth pit : diviners, soothsayers, and magicians. — Amphiaraus. — Tiresias. — Aruns. — Manto. — Eurypylus. — Michael Scott. — Asdente.

OF a new punishment needs must I make verses, and give material to the twentieth canto of the first lay, which is of the submerged.[1]

I was now wholly set on looking into the disclosed depth that was bathed with tears of anguish, and I saw folk coming, silent and weeping, through the circular valley, at the pace at which litanies go in this world. As my sight descended deeper among them, each appeared marvelously distorted from the chin to the beginning of the chest; for toward their reins their face was turned, and they must needs go backwards, because they were deprived of looking forward. Perchance sometimes by force of palsy one has been thus completely twisted, but I never saw it, nor do I think it can be.

So may God let thee, Reader, gather fruit from thy reading, now think for thyself how I could

[1] Plunged into the misery of Hell.

keep my face dry, when near by I saw our image so contorted that the weeping of the eyes
bathed the buttocks along the cleft.   Truly I wept,
leaning on one of the rocks of the hard crag, so
that my Guide said to me, "Art thou also one of
the fools ?   Here pity liveth when it is quite dead.[1]
Who is more wicked than he who feels compassion
at the Divine Judgment?   Lift up thy head, lift
up, and see him [2] for whom the earth opened before the eyes of the Thebans, whereon they shouted
all, ' Whither art thou rushing, Amphiaraus?
Why dost thou leave the war ? '   And he stopped
not from falling headlong down far as Minos, who
seizes hold of every one.   Look, how he has made a
breast of his shoulders !   Because he wished to see
too far before him, he looks behind and makes a
backward path.

   " See Tiresias,[3] who changed his semblance, when
from a male he became a female, his members all
of them being transformed ; and afterwards was

[1] It is impossible to give the full significance of Dante's words
in a literal translation, owing to the double meaning of *pietà* in
the original.
          Qui vive la pietà quando è ben morta.

That is: " Here liveth piety when pity is quite dead."
   [2] One of the seven kings who besieged Thebes, augur and
prophet.   Dante found his story in Statius, *Thebais*, viii. 84.
   [3] The Theban soothsayer.   Dante had learned of him from
Ovid., *Metam.*, iii. 320 *sqq.*, as well as from Statius.

obliged to strike once more the two entwined serpents with his rod, ere he could regain his masculine plumage. Aruns [1] is he that to this one's belly has his back, who on the mountains of Luni (where grubs the Carrarese who dwells beneath), amid white marbles, had a cave for his abode, whence for looking at the stars and the sea his view was not cut off.

"And she who with her loose tresses covers her breasts, which thou dost not see, and has on that side all her hairy skin, was Manto,[2] who sought through many lands, then settled there where I was born; whereof it pleases me that thou listen a little to me. After her father had departed from life, and the city of Bacchus had become enslaved, long while she wandered through the world. Up in fair Italy lies a lake, at foot of the alp that shuts in Germany above Tyrol, and it is called Benaco.[3] Through a thousand founts, I think, and more, between Garda and Val Camonica, the Apennine is bathed by the water which settles in that lake. Midway is a place where the Trentine Pastor and he of Brescia and the Veronese might

---

[1] An Etruscan haruspex of whom Lucan tells, —

Aruns incoluit desertae moenia Lunae.
Phars. i. 586.

[2] The daughter of Tiresias, of whom Statius, Ovid, and Virgil all tell.

[3] Now Lago di Garda.

each give his blessing if he took that road.[1]   Pes-
chiera, fortress fair and strong, sits to confront
the Brescians and Bergamasques, where the shore
round about is lowest.   Thither needs must fall
all that which in the lap of Benaco cannot stay,
and it becomes a river down through the verdant
pastures.   Soon as the water gathers head to run,
no longer is it called Benaco, but Mincio, far as
Governo, where it falls into the Po.   No long
course it hath before it finds a plain, on which it
spreads, and makes a marsh, and is wont in summer sometimes to be noisome.   Passing that way,
the cruel virgin saw a land in the middle of
the fen without culture and bare of inhabitants.
There, to avoid all human fellowship, she stayed
with her servants to practice her arts, and lived,
and left there her empty body.   Afterward the
men who were scattered round about gathered to
that place, which was strong because of the fen
which surrounded it.   They built the city over
those dead bones, and for her, who first had chosen
the place, they called it Mantua, without other au-
gury.   Of old its people were more thick within it,
before the stupidity of Casalodi had been tricked
by Pinamonte.[2]   Therefore I warn thee, that if

---

[1] Where the three dioceses meet.

[2] The Count of Casalodi, being lord of Mantua about 1276,
gave ear to the treacherous counsels of Messer Pinamonte de'
Buonacorsi, and was driven, with his friends, from the city.

thou ever hearest otherwise the origin of my town, no falsehood may defraud the truth."

And I, " Master, thy discourses are so certain to me, and so lay hold on my faith, that the others would be to me as dead embers. But tell me of the people who are passing, if thou seest any one of them worthy of note; for only unto that my mind reverts."

Then he said to me, " That one, who from his cheek stretches his beard upon his dusky shoulders, was an augur when Greece was so emptied of males that they scarce remained for the cradles, and with Calchas at Aulis he gave the moment for cutting the first cable. Eurypylus was his name, and thus my lofty Tragedy sings him in some place ;[1] well knowest thou this, who knowest the whole of it. That other who is so small in the flanks was Michael Scott,[2] who verily knew the game of magical deceptions. See Guido Bonatti,[3] see Asdente,[4] who now would wish he had attended

[1] Suspensi Eurypylum scitantem oracula Phoebi
Mittimus.   *Æneid*, ii. 112.

[2] A wizard of such dreaded fame
    That, when in Salamanca's cave
    Him listed his magic wand to wave,
The bells would ring in Notre Dame.
            Lay of the Last Minstrel, Canto ii.

[3] A famous astrologer of Forlì, in the thirteenth century.

[4] Dante, in the *Convito*, trattato iv. c. 16, says that if *noble*

to his leather and his thread, but late repents. See
the forlorn women who left the needle, the spool,
and the spindle, and became fortune-tellers ; they
wrought spells with herb and with image.

"But come on now, for already Cain with his
thorns [1] holds the confines of both the hemispheres,
and touches the wave below Seville. And already
yesternight was the moon round ; well shouldst
thou remember it, for it did thee no harm sometimes in the deep wood." Thus he spoke to me,
and we went on the while.

meant being widely known, then "Asdente, the shoemaker of
Parma, would be more noble than any of his fellow-citizens."

[1] The Man in the Moon, according to an old popular legend.

CANTO XXI.

So from bridge to bridge we went, speaking other things, which my Comedy careth not to sing, and held the summit, when we stopped to see the next cleft of Malebolge and the next vain lamentations ; and I saw it wonderfully dark.

As in the Arsenal of the Venetians, in winter, the sticky pitch for smearing their unsound vessels is boiling, because they cannot go to sea, and, instead thereof, one builds him a new bark, and one caulks the sides of that which hath made many a voyage ; one hammers at the prow, and one at the stern ; another makes oars, and another twists the cordage ; and one the foresail and the mainsail patches, — so, not by fire, but by divine art, a thick pitch was boiling there below, which belimed the bank on every side. I saw it, but saw not in it aught but the bubbles which the boiling raised, and all of it swelling up and again sinking compressed.

While I was gazing down there fixedly, my Leader, saying, "Take heed ! take heed !" drew me to himself from the place where I was standing. Then I turned as one who is slow to see what it behoves him to fly, and whom a sudden fear unnerves, and delays not to depart in order to see. And I saw behind us a black devil come running up along the crag. Ah! how fell he was in aspect, and how rough he seemed to me in action, with wings open, and light upon his feet! His shoulder, which was sharp and high, was laden by a sinner with both haunches, the sinew of whose feet he held clutched. " O Malebranche [1] of our bridge," he said, " lo, one of the Ancients of Saint Zita! [2] put him under, for I return again to that city, which I have furnished well with them ; every man there is a barrator,[3] except Bonturo : [4] there, for money, of No they make Ay." He hurled him down, and along the hard crag he turned, and never mastiff loosed was in such haste to follow a thief.

That one sank under, and came up back uppermost, but the demons that had shelter of the bridge cried out, " Here the Holy Face [5] avails not ;

[1] *Malebranche* means Evil-claws.

[2] One of the chief magistrates of Lucca, whose special protectress was Santa Zita.

[3] A corrupt official, selling justice or office for bribes ; in general, a peculator or cheat.

[4] Ironical.

[5] An image of Christ upon the cross, ascribed to Nicodemus, still venerated at Lucca.

here one swims otherwise than in the Serchio;[1] therefore, if thou dost not want our grapples, make no show above the pitch." Then they struck him with more than a hundred prongs, and said, " Covered must thou dance here, so that, if thou canst, thou mayst swindle secretly." Not otherwise cooks make their scullions plunge the meat with their hooks into the middle of the cauldron, so that it may not float.

The good Master said to me, " In order that it be not apparent that thou art here, crouch down behind a splinter, that may afford some screen to thee, and at any offense that may be done to me be not afraid, for I have knowledge of these things, because another time I was at such a fray."

Then he passed on beyond the head of the bridge, and when he arrived upon the sixth bank, he had need of a steadfast front. With such fury and with such storm, as dogs run out upon the poor wretch, who of a sudden begs where he stops, they came forth from under the little bridge, and turned against him all their forks. But he cried out, " Be no one of you savage; ere your hook take hold of me, let one of you come forward that he may hear me, and then take counsel as to grappling me." All cried out, " Let Malacoda[2] go ! "

---

[1] The river that runs not far from Lucca.

[2] Wicked tail.

Whereon one moved, and the rest stood still; and he came toward him, saying, "What doth this avail him?" "Thinkest thou, Malacoda, to see me come here," said my Master, "safe hitherto from all your hindrances, except by Will Divine and fate propitious? Let us go on, for in Heaven it is willed that I show another this savage road." Then was his arrogance so fallen that he let the hook drop at his feet, and said to the rest, "Now let him not be struck."

And my Leader to me, "O thou that sittest cowering among the splinters of the bridge, securely now return to me." Whereat I moved and came swiftly to him. And the devils all pressed forward, so that I feared they would not keep their compact. And thus I once saw the foot-soldiers afraid, who came out under pledge from Caprona,[1] seeing themselves among so many enemies. I drew with my whole body alongside my Leader, and turned not mine eyes from their look, which was not good. They lowered their forks, and, "Wilt thou that I touch him on the rump?" said one to the other, and they answered, "Yes, see thou nick it for him." But that demon who was holding speech with my Leader turned very quickly and said, "Stay, stay, Scarmiglione!"

[1] In August, 1290, the town of Caprona, on the Arno, surrendered to the Florentine troops, with whom Dante was serving.

Then he said to us, "Further advance along this
crag there cannot be, because the sixth arch lies all
shattered at the bottom. And if to go forward still
is your pleasure, go on along this rocky bank; near
by is another crag that affords a way. Yesterday,
five hours later than this hour, one thousand two
hundred and sixty-six years were complete since
the way was broken here.[1] I am sending thitherward some of these of mine, to see if any one is
airing himself; go ye with them, for they will not
be wicked. Come forward, Alichino and Calcabrina," began he to say, "and thou, Cagnazzo; and
do thou, Barbariccia, guide the ten. Let Libicocco come also, and Draghignazzo, tusked Ciriatto,
and Graffiacane, and Farfarello, and mad Rubicante. Search round about the boiling pitch; let
these be safe far as the next crag, that all un-
broken goes over these dens."

"O me! Master, what is it that I see?" said
I; "pray let us go alone without escort, if thou
knowest the way, for I desire it not for myself. If
thou art as wary as thou art wont to be, dost thou
not see that they show their teeth, and threaten
harm to us with their brows?" And he to me,
"I would not have thee afraid. Let them grin
on at their will, for they are doing it at the boiled
wretches."

---

[1] By the earthquake at the death of the Saviour.

Upon the left bank they wheeled round, but first each had pressed his tongue with his teeth toward their leader for a signal, and he had made a trumpet of his rump.

CANTO XXII.

Eighth Circle : fifth pit : barrators. — Ciampolo of Navarre. — Fra Gomita. — Michael Zanche. — Fray of the Malebranche.

I HAVE seen of old horsemen moving camp, and beginning an assault, and making their muster, and sometimes setting forth on their escape ; I have seen runners through your land, O Aretines, and I have seen freebooters starting, tournaments struck and jousts run, at times with trumpets, and at times with bells, with drums, and with signals from strongholds, and with native things and foreign, — but never with so strange a pipe did I see horsemen or footmen set forth, or ship by sign of land or star.

We went along with the ten demons. Ah, the fell company ! but in the church with saints, and in the tavern with gluttons. Ever on the pitch was I intent, to see every aspect of the pit, and of the people that were burning in it.

As dolphins, when, by the arching of their back, they give a sign to sailors that they take heed for the safety of their vessel, so, now and then, to alleviate his pain, one of the sinners showed his back and hid in less time than it lightens. And as at the edge of the water of a ditch the frogs stand with only their muzzle out, so that they conceal their feet and the rest of their bulk, thus stood on every side the sinners ; but as Barbariccia approached so did they draw back beneath the boiling. I saw, and still my heart shudders at it, one waiting, just as it happens that one frog stays and another jumps. And Graffiacane, who was nearest over against him, hooked him by his pitchy locks, and drew him up so that he seemed to me an otter. I knew now the name of every one of them, so had I noted them when they were chosen, and when they had called each other I had listened how. " O Rubicante, see thou set thy claws upon him so thou flay him," shouted all the accursed ones together.

And I, "My Master, see, if thou canst, that thou find out who is the luckless one come into the hands of his adversaries." My Leader drew up to his side, asked him whence he was, and he replied, " I was born in the kingdom of Navarre ; my mother placed me in service of a lord, for she had borne me to a ribald, destroyer of himself and of his substance. Afterward I was of the household of the good King Thibault ;[1] there I set myself to

---

[1] Probably Thibault II., the brother-in-law of St Louis, who accompanied him on his last disastrous crusade, and died on his way home in 1270.

practice barratry, for which I pay reckoning in this heat."

And Ciriatto, from whose mouth protruded on either side a tusk, as in a boar, made him feel how one of them rips. Among evil cats the mouse had come ; but Barbariccia clasped him in his arms, and said, "Stand off, while I enfork him," and to my Master turned his face. "Ask," said he, "if thou desirest to know more from him, before some other undo him." The Leader, "Now, then, tell of the other sinners ; knowst thou any one under the pitch who is Italian?" And he, "I parted short while since from one who was a neighbor to it ; would that with him I still were covered so that I might not fear claw or hook." And Libicocco said, "We have borne too much," and seized his arm with his grapple so that, tearing, he carried off a sinew of it. Draghignazzo, also, he wished to give him a clutch down at his legs, whereat their decurion turned round about with evil look.

When they were a little appeased, my Leader, without delay, asked him who still was gazing at his wound, "Who was he from whom thou sayest thou madest ill parting to come to shore?" And he replied, "It was Brother Gomita, he of Gallura,[1]

---

[1] Gallura, one of the four divisions of Sardinia, called judicatures, made by the Pisans, after their conquest of the island. The lord of Gomita was the gentle Judge Nino, whom Dante meets in Purgatory. Gomita was hung for his frauds.

vessel of all fraud, who held the enemies of his lord in hand, and dealt so with them that they all praise him for it. Money he took, and let them smoothly off, so he says; and in other offices besides he was no little barrator, but sovereign. With him frequents Don Michael Zanche of Logodoro,[1] and in talking of Sardinia their tongues feel not weary. O me! see ye that other who is grinning: I would say more, but I fear lest he is making ready to scratch my itch." And the grand provost, turning to Farfarello, who was rolling his eyes as if to strike, said, " Get thee away, wicked bird ! "

" If you wish to see or to hear Tuscans or Lombards," thereon began again the frightened one, " I will make them come; but let the Malebranche stand a little withdrawn, so that they may not be afraid of their vengeance, and I, sitting in this very place, for one that I am, will make seven of them come, when I shall whistle as is our wont to do whenever one of us comes out." Cagnazzo at this speech raised his muzzle, shaking his head, and said, " Hear the knavery he has devised for throwing himself under ! " Whereon he who had snares in great plenty answered, " Too knavish am I, when I procure for mine own companions greater sor-

---

[1] Logodoro was another of the judicatures of Sardinia. Don Michael Zanche was a noted man, but of his special sins little or nothing has been recorded by the chroniclers.

row." Alichino held not in, and, in opposition to the others, said to him, "If thou dive, I will not come behind thee at a gallop, but I will beat my wings above the pitch; let the ridge be left, and be the bank a shield, to see if thou alone availest more than we."

O thou that readest! thou shalt hear new sport. Each turned his eyes to the other side, he first who had been most averse to doing it. The Navarrese chose well his time, planted his feet firmly on the ground, and in an instant leaped, and from their purpose freed himself. At this, each of them was pricked with shame, but he most who was the cause of the loss; wherefore he started and cried out, "Thou art caught." But little it availed, for wings could not outstrip fear. The one went under, and the other, flying, turned his breast upward. Not otherwise the wild duck on a sudden dives when the falcon comes close, and he returns up vexed and baffled. Calcabrina, enraged at the flout, kept flying behind him, desirous that the sinner should escape, that he might have a scuffle; and when the barrator had disappeared he turned his talons upon his companion, and grappled with him above the ditch. But the other was indeed a sparrowhawk full grown to gripe him well, and both fell into the midst of the boiling pool. The heat was a sudden ungrappler, but nevertheless there was no rising from it, they had their wings so glued. Barbariccia, grieving with the rest of his troop, made four of them fly to the other side with all their forks, and very quickly, this side and that, they descended to their post. They stretched out their hooks toward the belimed ones, who were already baked within the crust : and we left them thus embroiled.

CANTO XXIII.

SILENT, alone, and without company, we went
on, one before, the other behind, as the Minor friars
go along the way. My thought was turned by the
present brawl upon the fable of Æsop, in which he
tells of the frog and the mole ; for *now* and *this
instant* are not more alike than the one is to the
other, if beginning and end are rightly coupled by
the attentive mind.[1]   And as one thought bursts
out from another, so from that then sprang another
which made my first fear double.   I reflected in
this wise : These through us have been flouted,
and with such harm and mock as I believe must

---

[1] " Sed dices forsan, lector," says Benvenuto da Imola, " nescio
per me videre quomodo istae duae fictiones habeant inter se tan-
tam convenientam.   Ad quod respondeo, quod passus vere est
fortis."   The point seems to be that, the frog having deceitfully
brought the mole to trouble and death, the mole declares, " me
vindicabit major," and the eagle swoops down and devours the
frog as well as the dead mole.   The comparison is not very close
except in the matter of anticipated vengeance.

vex them greatly ; if anger to ill-will be added,
they will come after us more merciless than the
dog upon the leveret which he snaps.

Already I was feeling my hair all bristling with
fear, and was backwards intent, when I said, " Master, if thou concealest not thyself and me speedily,
I am afraid of the Malebranche ; we have them
already behind us, and I so imagine them that I
already feel them." And he, " If I were of leaded
glass,[1] I should not draw thine outward image
more quickly to me than thine inward I receive.
Even now came thy thoughts among mine, with
similar action and with similar look, so that of
both one sole design I made. If it be that the
right bank lieth so that we can descend into the
next pit, we shall escape the imagined chase."

Not yet had he finished reporting this design,
when I saw them coming with spread wings, not
very far off, with will to take us. My Leader on
a sudden took me, as a mother who is wakened by
the noise, and near her sees the kindled flames,
who takes her son and flies, and, having more care
of him than of herself, stays not so long as only to
put on a shift. And down from the ridge of the
hard bank, supine he gave himself to the sloping
rock that closes one of the sides of the next pit.
Never ran water so swiftly through a duct, to turn

[1] A mirror.

the wheel of a land-mill, when it approaches near-est to the paddles, as my Master over that border, bearing me along upon his breast, as his own son, and not as his companion. Hardly had his feet reached the bed of the depth below, when they were on the ridge right over us; but here there was no fear, for the high Providence that willed to set them as ministers of the fifth ditch deprived them all of power of departing thence.

There below we found a painted people who were going around with very slow steps, weeping, and in their semblance weary and vanquished. They had cloaks, with hoods lowered before their eyes, made of the same cut as those of the monks in Cluny. Outwardly they are gilded, so that it dazzles, but within all lead, and so heavy that Frederick put them on of straw.[1] Oh mantle wearisome for eternity!

We turned, still ever to the left hand, along with them, intent on their sad plaint. But because of the weight that tired folk came so slowly that we had fresh company at every movement of the haunch. Wherefore I to my Leader, "See that thou find some one who may be known by deed or name, and so in going move thy eyes around."

---

[1] The leaden cloaks which the Emperor Frederick II. caused to be put on criminals, who were then burned to death, were light as straw in comparison with these.

And one who understood the Tuscan speech cried
out behind us, "Stay your feet, ye who run thus
through the dusky air; perchance thou shalt have
from me that which thou askest." Whereon the
Leader turned and said, "Await, and then according to his pace proceed." I stopped, and saw two
show, by their look, great haste of mind to be with
me, but their load delayed them, and the narrow
way.

When they had come up, somewhile, with eye
askance,[1] they gazed at me without a word; then
they turned to each other, and said one to the
other, "This one seems alive by the action of his
throat; and if they are dead, by what privilege do
they go uncovered by the heavy stole?" Then
they said to me, "O Tuscan, who to the college of
the wretched hypocrites art come, disdain not to tell
who thou art." And I to them, "I was born and
grew up on the fair river of Arno, at the great town;
and I am in the body that I have always had. But
ye, who are ye, in whom such woe distills, as I see,
down your cheeks? and what punishment is on you
that so sparkles?" And one of them replied to
me, "The orange hoods are of lead so thick that
the weights thus make their scales to creak. Jovial Friars[2] were we, and Bolognese; I Catalano,

---

[1] They could not raise their heads for a straight look.
[2] Brothers of the order of Santa Maria, established in 1261,

and he Loderingo named, and together taken by thy
city, as one man alone is wont to be taken, in order
to preserve its peace ; and we were such as still is
apparent round about the Gardingo." I began,
" O Friars, your evil " — but more I said not, for
there struck mine eyes one crucified with three
stakes on the ground. When me he saw he writhed
all over, blowing into his beard with sighs : and
the Friar Catalano, who observed it, said to me,
" That transfixed one, whom thou lookest at, coun-
seled the Pharisees that it was expedient to put one
man to torture for the people. Crosswise and
naked is he on the path, as thou seest, and he first
must feel how much whoever passes weighs. And
in such fashion his father-in-law is stretched in
this ditch, and the others of that Council which

with knightly vows and high intent. From their free life the
name of " Jovial Friars " was given to the members of the order.
After the battle of Montaperti (1260) the Ghibellines held the
upper hand in Florence for more than five years. The defeat and
death of Manfred early in 1266, at the battle of Benevento, shook
their power and revived the hopes of the Guelphs. As a measure
of compromise, the Florentine Commune elected two podestàs,
one from each party ; the Guelph was Catalano de' Malavolti, the
Ghibelline, Loderingo degli Andalò, both from Bologna. They
were believed to have joined hands for their own gain, and to have
favored the reviving power of the Guelphs. In the troubles of
the year the houses of the Uberti, a powerful Ghibelline family,
were burned. They lay in the region of the city called the Gardingo, close to the Palazzo Vecchio.

for the Jews was seed of ill." [1]   Then I saw Virgil
marvelling over him that was extended on a cross
so vilely in eternal exile.   Thereafter he addressed
this speech to the Friar, " May it not displease thee,
so it be allowed thee, to tell us if on the right hand
lies any opening whereby we two can go out without constraining any of the Black Angels to come
to deliver us from this deep."   He answered then,
" Nearer than thou hopest is a rock that from the
great encircling wall proceeds and crosses all the
savage valleys, save that at this one it is broken,
and does not cover it.   Ye can mount up over the
ruin that slopes on the side, and heaps up at the
bottom."   The Leader stood a little while with
bowed head, then said, " Ill he reported the matter,
he who hooks the sinners yonder." [2]   And the
Friar, " I once heard tell at Bologna vices enough
of the devil, among which I heard that he is false,
and the father of lies."   Then the Leader with
great steps went on, disturbed a little with anger in
his look ; whereon I departed from the heavily
burdened ones, following the prints of the beloved
feet.

[1] Annas " was father in law to Caiaphas, which was the high
priest that same year.   Now Caiaphas was he, which gave counsel
to the Jews, that it was expedient that one man should die for the
people."   John xviii. 13–14 ; *id.* xi. 47–50.

[2] Malacoda had told him that he would find a bridge not far
off by which to cross this sixth bolgia.

CANTO XXIV.

Eighth Circle. The poets climb from the sixth pit. — Seventh pit, filled with serpents, by which thieves are tormented. — Vanni Fucci. — Prophecy of calamity to Dante.

In that part of the young year when the sun tempers his locks beneath Aquarius,[1] and now the nights decrease toward half the day,[2] when the hoar frost copies on the ground the image of her white sister,[3] but the point of her pen lasts little while, the rustic, whose provision fails, gets up and sees the plain all whitened o'er, whereat he strikes his thigh, returns indoors, and grumbles here and there, like the poor wretch who knows not what to do; again goes out and picks up hope again, seeing the world to have changed face in short while, and takes his crook and drives forth his flock to pasture: in like manner the Master made me dismayed, when I saw his front so disturbed, and in like manner speedily arrived the plaster for the hurt. For when we came

---

[1] Toward the end of winter.

[2] Half of the twenty-four hours.

[3] The frost copies the look of the snow, but her pen soon loses its cut, that is, the white frost soon vanishes.

to the ruined bridge, the Leader turned to me with
that sweet look which I first saw at the foot of the
mount.[1] He opened his arms, after some counsel
taken with himself, looking first well at the ruin,
and laid hold of me. And as one who acts and con-
siders, who seems always to be ready beforehand,
so lifting me up toward the top of a great rock, he
took note of another splinter, saying, " Seize hold
next on that, but try first if it is such that it may
support thee." It was no way for one clothed in a
cloak, for we with difficulty, he light and I pushed
up, could mount from jag to jag. And had it not
been that on that precinct the bank was shorter
than on the other side, I do not know about him,
but I should have been completely overcome. But
because all Malebolge slopes toward the opening of
the lowest abyss, the site of each valley is such that
one side rises and the other sinks.[2] We came,
however, at length, up to the point where the last
stone is broken off. The breath was so milked
from my lungs when I was up that I could no
farther, but sat me down on first arrival.

"Now it behoves thee thus to put off sloth,"
said the Master, " for, sitting upon down or under

---

[1] The hill of the first Canto, at the foot of which Virgil had
appeared to Dante.

[2] The level of the whole circle slopes toward the central deep,
so that the inner side of each pit is of less height than the outer.

quilt, one attains not fame, without which he who consumes his life leaves of himself such trace on earth as smoke in air, or in water the foam. And therefore rise up, conquer the exhaustion with the spirit that conquers every battle, if by its heavy body it be not dragged down. A longer stairway needs must be ascended; it is not enough from these to have departed; if thou understandest me, now act so that it avail thee." Then I rose up, showing myself furnished better with breath than I felt, and said, " Go on, for I am strong and resolute."

Up along the crag we took the way, which was rugged, narrow, and difficult, and far steeper than the one before. I was going along speaking in order not to seem breathless, and a voice, unsuitable for forming words, came out from the next ditch. I know not what it said, though I was already upon the back of the arch that crosses here ; but he who was speaking seemed moved to anger. I had turned downwards, but living eyes could not go to the bottom, because of the obscurity. Wherefore I said, " Master, see that thou go on to the next girth, and let us descend the wall, for as from hence I hear and do not understand, so I look down and shape out nothing." " Other reply," he said, " I give thee not than doing, for an honest request ought to be followed by the deed in silence."

We descended the bridge at its head, where it joins on with the eighth bank, and then the pit was apparent to me. And I saw therewithin a terrible heap of serpents, and of such hideous look that the memory still curdles my blood. Let Libya with her sand vaunt herself no more; for though she brings forth chelydri, jaculi, and phareæ, and cenchri with amphisbœna, she never, with all Ethiopia, nor with the land that lies on the Red Sea, showed either so many plagues or so evil. •

Amid this cruel and most dismal store were running people naked and in terror, without hope of hole or heliotrope.[1] They had their hands tied behind with serpents, which fixed through the reins their tail and their head, and were knotted up in front.

And lo! at one, who was on our side, darted a serpent that transfixed him there where the neck is knotted to the shoulders. Nor *O* nor *I* was ever so quickly written as he took fire and burned, and all ashes it behoved him to become in falling. And when upon the ground he lay thus destroyed, the dust drew together of itself, and into that same one instantly returned. Thus by the great sages it is affirmed that the Phœnix dies, and then is reborn when to her five hundredth year she draws

[1] A precious stone, of green color, spotted with red, supposed to make its wearer invisible.

nigh. Nor herb nor grain she feeds on in her life, but only on tears of incense and on balsam, and nard and myrrh are her last winding-sheet.

And as he who falls and knows not how, by force of demon that drags him to ground, or of other attack that seizeth the man; when he arises and around him gazes, all bewildered by the great anguish that he has suffered, and in looking sighs, such was that sinner after he had risen. Oh power of God! how just thou art that showerest down such blows for vengeance!

The Leader asked him then who he was; whereon he answered, "I rained from Tuscany short time ago into this fell gullet. Bestial life, and not human, pleased me, like a mule that I was. I am Vanni Fucci, beast, and Pistoia was my fitting den." And I to my Leader, "Tell him not to budge, and ask what sin thrust him down here, for I have seen him a man of blood and rages." And the sinner who heard dissembled not, but directed toward me his mind and his face, and was painted with dismal shame. Then he said, "More it grieves me, that thou hast caught me in the misery where thou seest me, than when I was taken from the other life. I cannot refuse that which thou demandest. I am put so far down because I was robber of the sacristy with the fair furnishings, and falsely hitherto has it been as-

cribed to another.[1] But that thou enjoy not this
sight, if ever thou shalt be forth of these dark
places, open thine ears to my announcement and
hear.[2] Pistoia first strips itself of the Black, then
Florence renovates her people and her customs.
Mars draws a flame from Val di Magra wrapped
in turbid clouds, and with impetuous and bitter
storm shall it be opposed upon Campo Piceno,
where it shall suddenly rend the mist, so that every
White shall thereby be smitten. And this have I
said because it must grieve thee."

[1] Vanni Fucci robbed the rich sacristy of the Church of St.
James, the cathedral of Pistoia. Suspicion of the crime fell upon
others, who, though innocent, were put to torture and hung for it.

[2] The following verses refer under their dark imagery to the
two parties, the Black and the White, introduced from Pistoia, by
which Florence was divided in the early years of the fourteenth
century, and to their fightings. The prophecy is dismal to Dante,
because it was with the Whites, whose overthrow Vanni Fucci
foretells, that his own fortunes were linked.

CANTO XXV.

Eighth Circle : seventh pit : fraudulent thieves. — Cacus.
— Agnel Brunelleschi and others.

AT the end of his words the thief raised his
hands with both the figs,[1] crying, "Take that,
God! for at Thee I square them." Thenceforth
the serpents were my friends, for then one coiled
around his neck, as if it said, "I will not that thou
say more," and another round his arms and bound
them up anew, clinching itself so in front that he
could not give a shake with them. Ah Pistoia!
Pistoia! why dost thou not decree to make ashes
of thyself, so that thou mayest last no longer, since
in evil-doing thou surpassest thine own seed?[2]
Through all the dark circles of Hell I saw no
spirit against God so proud, not he who fell at
Thebes down from the walls.[3] He fled away and
spake no word more.

And I saw a Centaur full of rage come crying

---

[1] A vulgar mode of contemptuous defiance, thrusting out the
fist with the thumb between the first and middle finger.

[2] According to tradition, Pistoia was settled by the followers
of Catiline who escaped after his defeat.

[3] Capaneus ; see Canto xiv.

out, "Where is, where is that obdurate one?" I
do not think Maremma has so many snakes as he
had upon his croup up to where our semblance
begins.   On his shoulders behind the nape a
dragon with open wings was lying upon him, and
it sets on fire whomsoever it encounters.   My Master said, "This is Cacus, who beneath the rock of
Mount Aventine made oftentimes a lake of blood.
He goes not on one road with his brothers because
of the fraudulent theft he committed of the great
herd that was in his neighborhood; wherefor his
crooked deeds ceased under the club of Hercules,
who perhaps dealt him a hundred blows with it,
and he felt not ten."

While he was so speaking, and that one had run
by, lo! three spirits came below us, of whom neither I nor my Leader was aware till when they
cried out, "Who are ye?" whereon our story
stopped, and we then attended only unto them. I
did not recognize them, but it happened, as it is
wont to happen by chance, that one must needs
name the other, saying, "Cianfa, where can he
have stayed?" Whereupon I, in order that the
Leader should attend, put my finger upward from
my chin to my nose.

If thou art now, Reader, slow to credit that which
I shall tell, it will not be a marvel, for I who saw it
hardly admit it to myself.   As I was holding `my

brow raised upon them, lo ! a serpent with six feet darts in front of one, and grapples close to him. With his middle feet he clasped his paunch, and with his forward took his arms, then struck his fangs in one and the other cheek. His hinder feet he stretched upon the thighs, and put his tail between the two, and behind bent it up along the reins. Ivy was never so bearded to a tree, as the horrible beast through the other's limbs entwined his own. Then they stuck together as if they had been of hot wax, and mingled their color ; nor one nor the other seemed now that which it was ; even as before the flame, up along the paper a dark color proceeds which is not yet black, and the white dies away. The other two were looking on, and each cried, " O me ! Agnello, how thou changest ! Lo, now thou art neither two nor one ! " Now were the two heads become one, when there appeared to us two countenances mixed in one face wherein the two were lost. Of four [1] strips the two arms were made ; the thighs with the legs, the belly and the chest became members that were never seen before. Each original aspect there was cancelled ; both and neither the perverse image appeared, and such it went away with slow step.

As the lizard under the great scourge of the dog-

[1] The two fore feet of the dragon and the two arms of the man were melted into two strange arms.

days, changing from hedge to hedge, seems a flash,
if it crosses the way, so seemed, coming toward the
belly of the two others, a little fiery serpent, livid,
and black as a grain of pepper. And that part
whereby our nourishment is first taken it transfixed
in one of them, then fell down stretched out before
him. The transfixed one gazed at it, but said
nothing; nay rather, with feet fixed, he yawned
even as if sleep or fever had assailed him. He
looked at the serpent, and that at him; one through
his wound, the other through his mouth, smoked
violently, and their smoke met. Let Lucan henceforth be silent, where he tells of the wretched Sa-
bellus, and of Nasidius, and wait to hear that which
now is uttered. Let Ovid be silent concerning
Cadmus and Arethusa, for if, poetizing, he converts
him into a serpent and her into a fountain, I envy
him not; for two natures front to front never did
he transmute, so that both the forms were prompt
to exchange their matter. To one another they re-
sponded by such rules, that the serpent made his
tail into a fork, and the wounded one drew together
his feet. The legs and the very thighs with them
so stuck together, that in short while the juncture
made no sign that was apparent. The cleft tail
took on the shape that was lost there, and its skin
became soft, and that of the other hard. I saw
the arms draw in through the armpits, and the two

feet of the beast which were short lengthen out in
proportion as those shortened. Then the hinder
feet, twisted together, became the member that
man conceals, and the wretched one from his had
two [1] stretched forth.

While the smoke is veiling both with a new
color, and generates hair on the one, and from
the other strips it, one rose up, and the other
fell down, not however turning aside their pitiless lights,[2] beneath which each was changing his
visage. He who was erect drew his in toward the
temples, and, from the excess of material that came
in there, issued the ears on the smooth cheeks;
that which did not run backwards but was retained,
of its superfluity made a nose for the face, and
thickened the lips so far as was needful. He who
was lying down drives his muzzle forward, and
draws in his ears through his skull, as the snail
doth his horns. And his tongue, which erst was
united and fit for speech, cleaves itself, and the
forked one of the other closes up; and the smoke
stops. The soul that had become a brute fled hiss-
ing along the valley, and behind him the other
speaking spits. Then he turned upon him his new
shoulders, and said to the other,[3] " I will that

---

[1] Hinder feet.

[2] Glaring steadily at each other.

[3] The third of the three spirits, the only one unchanged.

Buoso[1] run, as I have done, groveling along this path."

Thus I saw the seventh ballast[2] change and re-change, and here let the novelty be my excuse, if my pen straggle[3] a little. And although my eyes were somewhat confused, and my mind bewildered, those could not flee away so covertly but that I clearly distinguished Puccio Sciancato, and he it was who alone, of the three companions that had first come, was not changed; the other[4] was he whom thou, Gaville, weepest.

[1] Buoso is he who has become a snake.

[2] The ballast, — the sinners in the seventh bolgia.

[3] Run into unusual detail.

[4] One Francesco Guercio de' Cavalcanti, who was slain by men of the little Florentine town of Gaville, and for whose death cruel vengeance was taken. The three who had first come were the three Florentine thieves, Agnello, Buoso, and Puccio. Cianfa Donati had then appeared as the serpent with six feet, and had been incorporated with Agnello. Lastly came Guercio Cavalcanti as a little snake, and changed form with Buoso.

CANTO XXVI.

Eighth Circle : eighth pit : fraudulent counselors. —
Ulysses and Diomed.

REJOICE, Florence, since thou art so great that
over sea and land thou beatest thy wings, and thy
name is spread through Hell. Among the thieves
I found five such, thy citizens, whereat shame comes
to me, and thou unto great honor risest not thereby.
But, if near the morning one dreams the truth, thou
shalt feel within little time what Prato, as well as
others, craves for thee.[1] And if now it were, it
would not be too soon. Would that it were so !
since surely it must be; for the more it will weigh
on me the more I age.

We departed thence, and up along the stairs that
the bourns[2] had made for our descent before, my
Leader remounted and dragged me. And pursuing
the solitary way mid the splinters and rocks of the
crag, the foot without the hand sped not. Then I
grieved, and now I grieve again when I direct my
mind to what I saw ; and I curb my genius more

---

[1] If that which I foresee is not a vain dream, the calamities
which thine enemies crave for thee will soon be felt.

[2] The projections of the rocky wall.

than I am wont, that it may not run unless virtue guide it; so that if a good star, or better thing, has given me of good, I may not grudge it to myself.

As the rustic who rests him on the hill in the season when he that brightens the world keepeth his face least hidden from us, what time the fly yieldeth to the gnat,[1] sees many fireflies down in the valley, perhaps there where he makes his vintage and ploughs, — with as many flames all the eighth pit was resplendent, as I perceived soon as I was there where the bottom became apparent. And as he[2] who was avenged by the bears saw the chariot of Elijah at its departure, when the horses rose erect to heaven, and could not so follow it with his eyes as to see aught save the flame alone, even as a little cloud, mounting upward: thus each[3] was moving through the gulley of the ditch, for not one shows its theft, and every flame steals away a sinner.[4]

I was standing on the bridge, risen up to look, so that if I had not taken hold of a rock I should have fallen below without being pushed. And the Leader, who saw me thus attent, said, "Within these fires are the spirits; each is swathed by that

---

[1] That is, in the summer twilight.

[2] Elisha. 2 Kings ii. 9-24.

[3] Of those flames.

[4] Within each flame a sinner was concealed.

wherewith he is enkindled." "My Master," I replied, "by hearing thee am I more certain, but
already I deemed that it was so, and already I
wished to say to thee, Who is in that fire that
cometh so divided at its top that it seems to rise
from the pyre on which Eteocles was put with his
brother?"[1] He answered me, "There within are
tormented Ulysses and Diomed, and thus together
they go in punishment, as of old in wrath.[2] And
within their flame they groan for the ambush of
the horse that made the gate, whence the gentle
seed of the Romans issued forth. Within it they
lament for the artifice whereby the dead Deidamia
still mourns for Achilles, and there for the Palladium they bear the penalty."[3] "If they can speak
within those sparkles," said I, "Master, much I

[1] Eteocles and Polynices, sons of Œdipus and Jocaste, who, con-
tending at the siege of Thebes, slew each other. Such was their
mutual hate that, when their bodies were burned on the same
funeral pile, the flames divided in two.

—exundant diviso vertice flammae
Alternosque apices abrupta luce coruscant.
Statius, Thebaid, xii. 431-2.

[2] Against the Trojans.

[3] It was through the stratagem of the wooden horse that Troy
was destroyed, and Æneas thus compelled to lead forth his followers who became the seed of the Romans. Deidamia was the
wife of Achilles, who slew herself for grief at his desertion and
departure for Troy, which had been brought about by the deceit
of Ulysses and Diomed. The Palladium was the statue of Athena,
on which the safety of Troy depended, stolen by the two heroes.

pray thee, and repray that the prayer avail a thousand, that thou make not to me denial of waiting till the horned flame come hither; thou seest that with desire I bend me toward it." And he to me, "Thy prayer is worthy of much praise, and therefore I accept it, but take heed that thy tongue restrain itself. Leave speech to me, for I have conceived what thou wishest, for, because they are Greeks, they would be shy, perchance, of thy words." [1]

When the flame had come there where it seemed to my Leader time and place, in this form I heard him speak to it: "O ye who are two within one fire, if I deserved of you while I lived, if I deserved of you much or little, when in the world I wrote the lofty verses, move not, but let one of you tell us, where, having lost himself, he went away to die." The greater horn of the ancient flame began to waver, murmuring, even as a flame that the wind wearies. Then moving its tip hither and thither, as it had been the tongue that would speak, it cast forth a voice, and said, —

"When I departed from Circe, who had retained me more than a year there near to Gaeta, before Æneas had so named it, neither fondness for my son, nor piety for my old father, nor the due

---

[1] The ancient heroes might be averse to talking with a man of the strange modern world.

love that should have made Penelope glad, could
overcome within me the ardor that I had to gain
experience of the world, and of the vices of men,
and of their valor. But I put forth on the deep,
open sea, with one vessel only, and with that little
company by which I had not been deserted. One
shore and the other [1] I saw as far as Spain, far as
Morocco and the island of Sardinia, and the rest
which that sea bathes round about. I and my companions were old and slow when we came to that
narrow strait where Hercules set up his bounds, to
the end that man may not put out beyond. [2] On
the right hand I left Seville, on the other already
I had left Ceuta. ' O brothers,' said I, ' who
through a hundred thousand perils have reached
the West, to this so little vigil of your senses that
remains be ye unwilling to deny the experience,
following the sun, of the world that hath no people.
Consider ye your origin; ye were not made to live
as brutes, but for pursuit of virtue and of knowledge.' With this little speech I made my companions so eager for the road that hardly afterwards
could I have held them back. And turning our
stern to the morning, with our oars we made wings
for the mad flight, always gaining on the left hand

---

[1] Of the Mediterranean.

[2] *Più oltre non;* the famous *Ne plus ultra,* adopted as his motto
by Charles V.

side. The night saw now all the stars of the other
pole, and ours so low that it rose not forth from
the ocean floor. Five times rekindled and as many
quenched was the light beneath the moon, since we
had entered on the deep pass, when there appeared
to us a mountain dim through the distance, and it
appeared to me so high as I had not seen any.
We rejoiced thereat, and soon it turned to lamentation, for from the strange land a whirlwind rose,
and struck the fore part of the vessel. Three times
it made her whirl with all the waters, the fourth
it made her stern lift up, and the prow go down,
as pleased Another, till the sea had closed over
us."

CANTO XXVII.

Eighth Circle : eighth pit : fraudulent counselors. —
Guido da Montefeltro.

Now was the flame erect and quiet, through
not speaking more, and now was going from us,
with the permission of the sweet poet, when another that was coming behind it made us turn our
eyes to its tip, by a confused sound that issued
forth therefrom. As the Sicilian bull [1] — that bel-
lowed first with the plaint of him (and that was
right) who had shaped it with his file — was wont
to bellow with the voice of the sufferer, so that, although it was of brass, yet it appeared transfixed
with pain, thus, through not at first having way
or outlet from the fire, the disconsolate words were
converted into its language. But when they had
taken their course up through the point, giving it
that vibration which the tongue had given in their
passage, we heard say, " O thou, to whom I direct

[1] The brazen bull of Phalaris, tyrant of Agrigentum, made to
hold criminals to be burned within it. Perillus, its inventor, was
the first to suffer. So these sinners are wrapped in the flames
which their fraudulent counsels had prepared for them.

my voice, thou that wast just speaking Lombard,[1]
saying, ' Now go thy way, no more I urge thee,'
although I may have arrived perchance somewhat
late, let it not irk thee to stop to speak with me,
behold, it irks not me, and I am burning.   If thou
but now into this blind world art fallen from that
sweet Italian land whence I bring all my sin, tell
me if the Romagnuoli have peace or war ; for I was
from the mountains there between Urbino and the
chain from which Tiber is unlocked." [2]

I was still downward attent and leaning over
when my Leader touched me on the side, saying,
" Speak thou, this is an Italian."   And I, who even
now had my answer ready, without delay began
to speak, " O soul, that art hidden there below, thy
Romagna is not, and never was, without war in the
hearts of her tyrants, but open war none have I
left there now.   Ravenna is as it hath been for
many years ; the eagle of Polenta[3] is brooding
there, so that he covers Cervia with his wings.

---

[1] Lombard, because the words were those of Virgil, whose
" parents were Lombards," and in speaking he had used a form
peculiar to the Lombard dialect.

[2] It is the spirit of the Ghibelline count, Guido da Montefeltro,
a famous freebooting captain, who speaks.

[3] Guido Novello da Polenta had been lord of Ravenna since
1275. He was father of Francesca da Rimini, and a friend of
Dante. His shield bore an eagle, gules, on a field, or. Cervia is
a small town on the coast, not far from Ravenna.

The city [1] that made erewhile the long struggle, and
of the French a bloody heap, finds itself again
beneath the green paws.   And the old mastiff and
the new of Verrucchio,[2] who made the ill disposal
of Montagna, make an auger of their teeth there
where they are wont.   The little lion of the white
lair [3] governs the city of Lamone and of Santerno,
and changes side from summer to winter.   And
she [4] whose flank the Savio bathes, even as she sits
between the plain and the mountain, lives between
tyranny and a free state.   Now who thou art, I
pray thee that thou tell us; be not harder than
another hath been,[5] so may thy name in the world
hold front."

   After the fire had somewhat roared according to
its fashion, the sharp point moved this way and

   [1] Forlì, where in 1282 Guido da Montefeltro had defeated, with
great slaughter, a troop, largely of French soldiers, sent against
him by Pope Martin III. It was now ruled by the Ordelaffi,
whose shield, party per fess, bore on its upper half, or, a demi-
lion, vert.

   [2] Malatesta, father and son, rulers of Rimini; father and brother of the husband and of the lover of Francesca da Rimini.
They had cruelly put to death Montagna di Parcitade, the head
of the Ghibellines of Rimini; and they ruled as tyrants, sucking
the blood of their subjects.

   [3] This is Maghinardo da Susinana, who bore a lion azure on a
field argent.

   [4] The city of Cesena.

   [5] Refuse not to answer me as I have answered thee.

that, and then gave forth this breath : " If I could
believe that my answer might be to a person who
should ever return unto the world, this flame would
stand without more quiverings ; but inasmuch as,
if I hear truth, never from this depth did any living man return, without fear of infamy I answer
thee.

" I was a man of arms, and then became a
cordelier, trusting, thus girt, to make amends ; and
surely my trust had been fulfilled but for the Great
Priest,[1] whom may ill betide ! who set me back into
my first sins ; and how and wherefore, I will that
thou hear from me. While I was that form of
bone and flesh that my mother gave me, my works
were not leonine, but of the fox. The wily practices, and the covert ways, I knew them all, and I
so plied their art that to the earth's end the sound
went forth. When I saw me arrived at that part
of my age where every one ought to strike the sails
and to coil up the ropes, what erst was pleasing to
me then gave me pain, and I yielded me repentant
and confessed. Alas me wretched ! and it would
have availed. The Prince of the new Pharisees
having war near the Lateran,[2] — and not with Saracens nor with Jews, for every enemy of his was
Christian, and none of them had been to conquer

---

[1] Boniface VIII.

[2] With the Colonna family, whose stronghold was Palestrina.

Acre,[1] nor a trafficker in the land of the Soldan, — regarded in himself neither his supreme office, nor the holy orders, nor in me that cord which is wont to make those girt with it more lean; but as Constantine besought Sylvester within Soracte to cure his leprosy,[2] so this one besought me as master to cure his proud fever. He asked counsel of me, and I kept silence, because his words seemed drunken. And then he said to me, 'Let not thy heart mistrust; from now I absolve thee, and do thou teach me to act so that I may throw Palestrina to the ground. Heaven can I lock and unlock, as thou knowest; for two are the keys that my predecessor held not dear.'[3] Then his grave arguments pushed me to where silence seemed to me the worst, and I said, 'Father, since thou washest me of that sin wherein I now must fall, long promise with short keeping will make thee triumph on the High Seat.' Francis[4] came for me afterwards, when I was dead, but one of the Black Cherubim said to him, 'Bear him not away; do me not wrong; he must come down among my

---

[1] Not one had been a renegade, to help the Saracens at the siege of Acre in 1291.

[2] It was for this service that Constantine was supposed to have made Sylvester "the first rich Father." See Canto xiv.

[3] His predecessor, Celestine V., had renounced the papacy.

[4] St. Francis came for his soul, as that of one of the brethren of his Order.

drudges because he gave the fraudulent counsel,
since which till now I have been at his hair;
for he who repents not cannot be absolved, nor
can repentance and will exist together, because of
the contradiction that allows it not.' O woeful
me! how I shuddered when he took me, saying
to me, 'Perhaps thou didst not think that I was
a logician.' To Minos he bore me; and he
twined his tail eight times round his hard back,
and, after he had bitten it in great rage, he said,
'This is one of the sinners of the thievish fire.'
Therefore I, where thou seest, am lost, and going
thus robed I rankle." When he had thus com-
pleted his speech the flame, sorrowing, departed,
twisting and flapping its sharp horn.

We passed onward, I and my Leader, along the
crag, far as upon the next arch that covers the
ditch in which the fee is paid by those who, sowing discord, win their burden.

CANTO XXVIII.

Eighth Circle : ninth pit : sowers of discord and schism.
— Mahomet and Ali. — Fra Dolcino. — Pier da Medicina. —
Curio. — Mosca. — Bertran de Born.

WHO, even with words unfettered,[1] could ever tell in full of the blood and of the wounds that I now saw, though many times narrating? Every tongue assuredly would come short, by reason of our speech and our memory that have small capacity to comprise so much.

If all the people were again assembled, that of old upon the fateful land of Apulia lamented for their blood shed by the Trojans,[2] and in the long war that made such high spoil of the rings,[3] as Livy writes, who erreth not; with those that, by resisting Robert Guiscard,[4] felt the pain of blows, and the rest whose bones are still heaped up at Ceperano,[5] where every Apulian was false, and

[1] In prose.

[2] The Romans, descendants of the Trojans.

[3] The spoils of the battle of Cannæ, in the second Punic War.

[4] The Norman conqueror and Duke of Apulia. He died in 1085.

[5] Where, in 1266, the leaders of the army of Manfred, King of Apulia and Sicily, treacherously went over to Charles of Anjou.

there by Tagliacozzo,[1] where without arms the old
Alardo conquered, — and one should show his limb
pierced through, and one his lopped off, it would
be nothing to equal the grisly mode of the ninth pit.

Truly cask, by losing mid-board or cross-piece, is
not so split open as one I saw cleft from the chin
to where the wind is broken : between his legs were
hanging his entrails, his inner parts were visible,
and the dismal sack that makes ordure of what is
swallowed.   Whilst all on seeing him I fix myself,
he looked at me, and with his hands opened his
breast, saying, " Now see how I rend myself, see
how mangled is Mahomet.   Ali[2] goeth before me
weeping, cleft in the face from chin to forelock ;
and all the others whom thou seest here were, when
living, sowers of scandal and of schism, and therefore are they so cleft.   A devil is here behind, that
adjusts us so cruelly, putting again to the edge of
the sword each of this crew, when we have turned
the doleful road, because the wounds are closed
up ere one passes again before him.   But thou,
who art thou, that musest on the crag, perchance
to delay going to the punishment that is adjudged

---

[1] Here, in 1265, Conradin, the nephew of Manfred, was defeated and taken prisoner. The victory was won by a stratagem
devised by Count Erard de Valéry.

[2] Cousin and son-in-law of Mahomet, and himself the head of
a schism.

on thine own accusations?"[1] "Nor death hath reached him yet," replied my Master, "nor doth sin lead him to torment him; but, in order to give him full experience, it behoves me, who am dead, to lead him through Hell down here, from circle to circle; and this is true as that I speak to thee."

More than a hundred there were that, when they heard him, stopped in the ditch to look at me, forgetting the torment in their wonder.

"Now, say to Fra Dolcino,[2] then, thou who perchance shalt shortly see the sun, if he wish not soon to follow me here, so to arm himself with supplies that stress of snow bring not the victory to the Novarese, which otherwise to gain would not be easy:" — after he had lifted one foot to go on Mahomet said to me these words, then on the ground he stretched it to depart.

Another who had his throat pierced and his nose cut off up under his brows, and had but one ear only, having stopped to look in wonder with the rest, before the rest opened his gullet, which outwardly was all crimson, and said, "O thou whom sin condemns not, and whom of old I saw above in the

[1] When the soul appears before Minos, every sin is confessed. See Canto V.

[2] A noted heretic and reformer, who for two years maintained himself in Lombardy against the forces of the Pope, but finally, being reduced by famine in time of snow, in 1307, was taken captive and burnt at Novara.

Latian land, if too great resemblance deceive me
not, remember Pier da Medicina [1] if ever thou return to see the sweet plain that from Vercelli slopes
to Marcabò, and make known to the two best of
Fano, to Messer Guido and likewise to Angiolello,[2]
that, if foresight here be not vain, they will be
cast forth from their vessel and drowned near to
the Cattolica, by treachery of a fell tyrant.   Between the islands of Cyprus and Majorca Neptune
never saw so great a crime, not of the pirates, nor
of the Argolic people.   That traitor who sees only
with one eye, and holds the city from sight of which
one who is here with me would fain have fasted,[3]
will make them come to parley with him; then will
act so that against the wind of Focara [4] they will not
need or vow or prayer."   And I to him, " Show
to me and declare, if thou wishest that I carry
up news of thee, who is he of the bitter sight?" [5]
Then he put his hand on the jaw of one of his
companions, and opened the mouth of him, crying,

---

[1] Medicina is a town in the Bolognese district.   Piero was a fos-
terer of discord.

[2] Guido del Cassero and Angiolello da Cagnano, treacherously
drowned by order of the one-eyed Malatestino, lord of Rimini.

[3] The city of Rimini, which Curio would wish never to have
seen.

[4] A high foreland near the Cattolica, between Rimini and Fano,
whence often fell dangerous squalls.

[5] He to whom the sight of Rimini had been bitter.

"This is he, and he speaks not; this outcast stifled
the doubt in Cæsar, by affirming that the man prepared always suffered harm from delay." Oh, how
dismayed, with his tongue slit in his gorge, seemed
to me Curio,[1] who in speech had been so hardy!

And one who had both hands lopped off, lifting
the stumps through the murky air so that the blood
made his face foul, cried out, "Thou shalt remember Mosca,[2] too, who said, alas! 'Thing done has
an end,' which was the seed of ill for the Tuscan
people." And I added thereto, "And death to
thine own race." Whereat he, accumulating woe
on woe, went away like a person sad and dis-
tracted.

But I remained to look at the crowd, and I saw
a thing that I should be afraid, without more proof,
only to tell, were it not that conscience reassures
me, the good companion that emboldens man under the hauberk of feeling himself pure. I saw

---

[1] Curio the Tribune, banished from Rome, fled to Cæsar delay-
ing to cross the Rubicon, and urged him on, with the argument,
according to Lucan, "*Tolle moras, semper nocuit differre paratis.*"
Phars. i. 281.

[2] In 1215 one of the Buondelmonti, plighted to a maiden of the
Amidei, broke faith, and engaged himself to a damsel of the Donati. The family of the girl who had been thus slighted took
counsel how to avenge the affront, and Mosca de' Lamberti gave
the ill advice to murder the young Buondelmonte. The murder
was the beginning of long woe to Florence, and of the division
of her people into Guelphs and Ghibellines.

in truth, and still I seem to see it, a trunk without a head going along even as the others of the dismal flock were going. And it was holding the cut-off head by its hair, dangling in hand like a lantern. And it gazed on us, and said, "O me!" Of itself it was making for itself a lamp; and they were two in one, and one in two. How it can be He knows who so ordains. When it was right at the foot of the bridge, it lifted its arm high with the whole head, in order to approach its words to us, which were, "Now see the dire punishment, thou that, breathing, goest seeing the dead: see thou if any other is great as this! And that thou mayest carry news of me, know that I am Bertran de Born,[1] he that gave to the young king the ill encouragements. I made father and son rebellious to each other. Ahithophel did not more with Absalom and with David by his wicked goadings. Because I divided persons so united, I bear my brain, alas! divided from its source which is in this trunk. Thus retaliation is observed in me."

[1] The famous troubadour who incited the young Prince Henry to rebellion against his father, Henry II. of England. The prince died in 1183.

CANTO XXIX.

Eighth Circle : ninth pit. — Geri del Bello. — Tenth pit :
falsifiers of all sorts. — Griffolino of Arezzo. — Capocchio.

THE many people and the diverse wounds had so
inebriated mine eyes that they were fain to stay
for weeping. But Virgil said to me, "What art
thou still watching? why is thy sight still fixed
down there among the dismal mutilated shades?
Thou hast not done so at the other pits; consider
if thou thinkest to count them, that the valley circles two and twenty miles ; and already the moon
is beneath our feet; the time is little now that is
conceded to us, and other things are to be seen
than thou seest." "If thou hadst," replied I
thereupon, "attended to the reason why I was
looking perhaps thou wouldst have permitted me
yet to stay."

Meanwhile my Leader went on, and I behind
him went, already making reply, and adding,
"Within that cavern where I just now was holding
my eyes so fixedly, I think that a spirit of my
own blood weeps the sin that down there costs so
dear." Then said the Master, "Let not thy

thought henceforth reflect on him; attend to other
thing, and let him there remain, for I saw him at
the foot of the little bridge pointing at thee, and
threatening fiercely with his finger, and I heard
him called Geri del Bello.[1]   Thou wert then so
completely engaged on him who of old held Hautefort[2] that thou didst not look that way till he had
departed." "O my Leader," said I, "the violent
death which is not yet avenged for him by any who
is sharer in the shame made him indignant, wherefore, as I deem, he went on without speaking
to me, and thereby has he made me pity him the
more."

Thus we spake far as the place on the crag
which first shows the next valley, if more light
were there, quite to the bottom.   When we were
above the last cloister of Malebolge so that its lay
brothers could appear to our sight, divers lamentations pierced me, that had their arrows barbed
with pity; wherefore I covered my ears with my
hands.

Such pain as there would be if, between July
and September, from the hospitals of Valdichiana
and of Maremma and of Sardinia[3] the sick should

---

[1] A cousin or uncle of Dante's father, of whom little is known
but what may be inferred from Dante's words and from the place
he assigns him in Hell.

[2] Bertran de Born, lord of Hautefort.

[3] Unhealthy regions, noted for the prevalence of malarial fevers
in summer.

all be in one ditch together, such was there here;
and such stench came forth therefrom, as is wont
to come from putrescent limbs. We descended
upon the last bank of the long crag, ever to the
left hand, and then my sight became more vivid
down toward the bottom, where the ministress of
the High Lord — infallible Justice — punishes the
falsifiers whom on earth she registers.

I do not think it was a greater sorrow to see the
whole people in Egina sick, when the air was so
full of pestilence that the animals, even to the little
worm, all fell dead (and afterwards the ancient
people, according as the poets hold for sure, were
restored by seed of ants), than it was to see the
spirits languishing in different heaps through that
dark valley. This one over the belly, and that over
the shoulders of another was lying, and this one,
crawling, was shifting himself along the dismal path.
Step by step we went without speech, looking at and
listening to the sick, who could not lift their persons.

I saw two seated leaning on each other, as pan
is leaned against pan to warm, spotted from head
to foot with scabs; and never did I see currycomb
plied by a boy for whom his lord is waiting nor by
one who keeps awake unwillingly, as each often
plied the bite of his nails upon himself, because of
the great rage of his itching which has no other
relief. And the nails dragged down the scab, even

as a knife the scales of bream or of other fish that
may have them larger.

"O thou, that with thy fingers dost dismail thyself," began my Leader unto one of them, "and
who sometimes makest pincers of them, tell me if
any Latian [1] is among those who are here within:
so may thy nails suffice thee eternally for this
work." "Latians are we whom here thou seest
so defaced, both of us," replied one weeping, "but
thou, who art thou that hast asked of us?" And
the Leader said, " I am one that descends with this
living man down from ledge to ledge, and I intend
to show Hell to him." Then their mutual support was broken; and trembling each turned to
me, together with others that heard him by re-
bound. The good Master inclined himself wholly
toward me, saying, " Say to them what thou wilt;"
and I began, since he was willing, " So may memory of you not steal away in the first world from
human minds, but may it live under many suns,
tell me who ye are, and of what race ; let not your
disfiguring and loathsome punishment fright you
from disclosing yourselves unto me." " I was from
Arezzo," replied one of them,[2] "and Albero of Siena had me put in the fire; but that for which I
died brings me not here. True it is that I said to

---

[1] Italian.

[2] This is supposed to be one Griffolino, of whom nothing is
known but what Dante tells.

him, speaking in jest, I knew how to raise myself
through the air in flight, and he, who had vain desire and little wit, wished that I should show him
the art, and only because I did not make him
Daedalus, made me be burned by one [1] that held
him as a son; but to the last pit of the ten, for
the alchemy that I practiced in the world, Minos,
to whom it is not allowed to err, condemned me."
And I said to the Poet, " Now was ever people so
vain as the Sienese? surely not so the French by
much." Whereon the other leprous one, who heard
me, replied to my words, " Except [2] Stricca who
knew how to make moderate expenditure, and Nic-
colò, who first invented the costly custom of the
clove [3] in the garden where such seed takes root;
and except the brigade in which Caccia of Asciano
wasted his vineyard and his great wood, and the
Abbagliato showed his wit. But that thou mayest
know who thus seconds thee against the Sienese,
so sharpen thine eye toward me that my face may
answer well to thee, so shalt thou see that I am the
shade of Capocchio, who falsified the metals by
alchemy; and thou shouldst recollect, if I descry
thee aright, how I was a good ape of nature."

[1] The Bishop of Siena.

[2] Ironical; these youths all being members of the company
known as the *brigata godereccia* or *spendereccia*, the joyous or
spendthrift brigade.

[3] The use of rich and expensive spices in cookery.

CANTO XXX.

Eighth Circle : tenth pit : falsifiers of all sorts. — Myrrha. — Gianni Schicchi. — Master Adam. — Sinon of Troy.

AT the time when Juno was wroth because of Semele against the Theban blood, as she showed more than once, Athamas became so insane, that seeing his wife come laden on either hand with her two sons, cried out, "Spread we the nets, so that I may take the lioness and the young lions at the pass," and then he stretched out his pitiless talons, taking the one who was named Learchus, and whirled him and struck him on a rock; and she drowned herself with her other burden. And when Fortune turned downward the all-daring loftiness of the Trojans, so that together with the kingdom the king was undone, Hecuba, sad, wretched, and captive, when she saw Polyxena dead, and woeful descried her Polydorus on the sea-bank, frantic, barked like a dog, — to such degree had grief distraught her mind.

But neither the furies of Thebes, nor the Trojan, were ever seen toward any one so cruel, whether in goading beasts or human limbs,[1] as I saw two shades pallid and naked who, biting, were running in the way that a boar does when from the sty he breaks loose. One came at Capocchio, and on the nape of his neck struck his teeth, so that dragging him he made his belly scratch along the solid bottom. And the Aretine,[2] who remained trembling, said to me, " That goblin is Gianni Schicchi, and rabid he goes thus maltreating others." " Oh," said I to him, " so may the other not fix his teeth on thee, let it not weary thee to tell who it is ere it start hence." And he to me, " That is the ancient soul of profligate Myrrha, who became her father's lover beyond rightful love. She came to sinning with him by falsifying herself in another's form, even as the other, who goes off there, undertook, in order to gain the lady of the herd,[3] to counterfeit Buoso Donati, making a will and giving to the will due form."

And after the two rabid ones upon whom I had

---

[1] No mad rages were ever so merciless as those of these furious spirits.

[2] Griffolino.

[3] Buoso Donati had died without making a will, whereupon his nephew suborned Gianni Schicchi to personate the dead man in bed, and to dictate a will in his favor. This Gianni did, but with a clause leaving to himself a favorite mare of Buoso's, the best in all Tuscany.

kept my eye had disappeared, I turned it to look
at the other miscreants. I saw one made in fashion
of a lute, had he but only had his groin cut off at
the part where man is forked. The heavy hy-
dropsy which, with the humor that it ill digests, so
unmates the members that the face corresponds not
with the belly, was making him hold his lips open
as the hectic does, who for thirst turns one toward
his chin, the other upward.

"Oh ye, who are without any punishment, and I
know not why, in the dismal world," said he to
us, "look and attend to the misery of Master
Adam. Living, I had enough of what I wished,
and now, alas! I long for a drop of water. The
rivulets that from the green hills of the Casentino
descend into the Arno, making their channels cool
and soft, stand ever before me, and not in vain ; for
their image dries me up far more than the disease
which strips my face of flesh. The rigid justice ·
that scourges me draws occasion from the place
where I sinned to put my sighs the more in flight.
There is Romena, where I falsified the alloy stamped
with the Baptist,[1] for which on earth I left my
body burned. But if here I could see the wretched
soul of Guido or of Alessandro, or of their brother,[2]

[1] The florin which bore on the obverse the figure of John the
Baptist, the protecting saint of Florence.
[2] Counts of Romena.

for Fount Branda[1] I would not give the sight. One of them is here within already, if the raging shades who go around speak true. But what does it avail me who have my limbs bound? If I were only yet so light that in a hundred years I could go an inch, I should already have set out along the path, seeking for him among this disfigured folk, although it circles round eleven miles, and is not less than half a mile across. Because of them I am among such a family; they induced me to strike the florins that had full three carats of base metal." And I to him, "Who are the two poor wretches that are smoking like a wet hand in winter, lying close to your confines on the right?" "Here I found them," he answered, "when I rained down into this trough, and they have not since given a turn, and I do not believe they will give one to all eternity. One is the false woman that accused Joseph, the other is the false Sinon the Greek, from Troy; because of their sharp fever they throw out such great reek."

And one of them who took it ill perchance at being named so darkly, with his fist struck him on his stiff paunch; it sounded as if it were a drum; and Master Adam struck him on the face with his arm that did not seem less hard, saying to him, "Though, because of my heavy limbs, moving

---

[1] The noted fountain in Siena, or perhaps one in Romena.

hence be taken from me, I have an arm free for such need." Whereon he replied, " When thou wast going to the fire thou hadst it not thus ready, but so and more thou hadst it when thou wast coining." And the hydropic, " Thou sayst true in this, but thou wast not so true a witness there where thou wast questioned of the truth at Troy." " If I spake false, thou didst falsify the coin," said Sinon, " and I am here for a single sin, and thou for more than any other demon." " Remember, perjured one, the horse," answered he who had the puffed up paunch, " and be it ill for thee that the whole world knows it." " And be ill for thee the thirst which cracks thy tongue," said the Greek, " and the putrid water that makes thy belly thus a hedge before thine eyes." Then the coiner, " So yawns thy mouth for its own harm as it is wont, for if I am thirsty, and humor stuffs me out, thou hast the burning, and the head that pains thee, and to lick the mirror of Narcissus thou wouldst not want many words of invitation."

To listen to them was I wholly fixed, when the Master said to me, " Now then look, for it wants but little that I quarrel with thee." When I heard him speak to me with anger, I turned me toward him with such shame that still it circles through my memory. And as is he that dreams of his harm, and, dreaming, desires to dream, so that

that which is he craves as if it were not, such I
became, not being able to speak, for I desired to
excuse myself, and I was indeed excusing myself,
and did not think that I was doing it. "Less shame
doth wash away a greater fault than thine hath
been," said the Master; "therefore disburden thyself of all regret, and make reckoning that I am
always at thy side, if again it happen that fortune
find thee where people are in similar brawl; for
the wish to hear it is a base wish."

CANTO XXXI.

The Giants around the Eighth Circle. — Nimrod. — Ephialtes. — Antæus sets the Poets down in the Ninth Circle.

ONE and the same tongue first stung me, so that
it tinged both my cheeks, and then supplied the
medicine to me. Thus do I hear[1] that the lance of
Achilles and of his father was wont to be cause
first of a sad and then of a good gift.

We turned our back to the wretched valley,[2] up
along the bank that girds it round, crossing without any speech. Here it was less than night and
less than day, so that my sight went little forward ; but I heard a horn sounding so loud that it
would have made every thunder faint, which directed my eyes, following its course counter to it,[3]
wholly to one place.

[1] Probably from Ovid, who more than once refers to the magic
power of the spear which had been given to Peleus by Chiron.
Shakespeare too had heard of it, and applies it, precisely as Dante
does, to one

> Whose smile and frown, like to Achilles' spear,
> Is able with the charge to kill and cure.
>
> 2 *Henry* VI. v. i.

[2] The tenth and last pit.

[3] My eyes went in the direction whence the sound came.

After the dolorous rout when Charlemagne lost
the holy gest, Roland sounded not so terribly.[1]
Shortwhile did I carry my head turned thitherward,
when it seemed to me I saw many high towers;
whereon I, "Master, say, what city is this?" And
he to me, "Because too far away thou peerest
through the darkness, it happens that thou dost err
in thy imagining. Thou shalt see well, if thou
arrivest there, how much the sense at distance is
deceived; therefore somewhat more spur thyself
on." Then tenderly he took me by the hand, and
said, "Before we go further forward, in order that
the fact may seem less strange to thee, know that
they are not towers, but giants, and they are in the
abyss [2] round about the bank, from the navel downward, one and all of them."

As when the mist is dissipating, the look little
by little shapes out what the vapor that thickens
the air conceals, so, as I pierced the gross and dark
air as we drew nearer and nearer to the verge, error
fled from me and fear grew upon me. For as above

---

[1] At Roncesvalles.

> Rollanz ad mis l'olifan à sa buche,
> Empeint le bien, par grant vertut le sunet.
> Halt sunt li pui e la voiz est mult lunge,
> Granz xxx. liwes l'oïrent-il respundre,
> Carles l'oït e ses cumpaignes tutes.
> > *Chanson de Roland*, 1753-57.

[2] The central deep of Hell, dividing the eighth circle from the
ninth, — the lowest.

its circular enclosure Montereggione [1] crowns itself
with towers, so with half their body the horrible
giants, whom Jove still threatens from heaven when
he thunders, betowered the bank that surrounds
the abyss.

And I discerned now the face of one, his shoulders, and his breast, and great part of his belly,
and down along his sides both his arms. Nature,
surely, when she left the art of such like creatures,
did exceeding well in taking such executers from
Mars; and if she repent not of elephants and of
whales, he who looks subtly holds her more just
and more discreet therefor; [2] for where the faculty
of the mind is added to evil will and to power, the
human race can make no defense against it. His
face seemed to me long and huge as the pine-cone [3]
of St. Peter at Rome, and in its proportion were
his other bones; so that the bank, which was an
apron from his middle downward, showed of him
fully so much above, that to reach to his hair three
Frieslanders [4] would have made ill vaunt. For I

[1] The towers of Montereggione in ruin still crown its broken
wall, and may be seen from the railroad not far from Siena, on
the way to Florence.

[2] For no longer creating giants.

[3] Of bronze, that came from the Mausoleum of Hadrian, and
in Dante's time stood in the fore-court of St. Peter's, and is now
in the Vatican gardens.

[4] Supposed to be tall men.

saw of him thirty great palms down from the place where one buckles his cloak.

"*Raphel mai amech zabi almi,*" the fierce mouth, to which sweeter psalms were not befitting, began to cry. And my Leader toward him, "Foolish soul! Keep to thy horn, and with that vent thyself when anger or other passion touches thee; seek at thy neck, and thou wilt find the cord that holds it tied, O soul confused! and see it lying athwart thy great breast." Then he said to me, "He himself accuses himself; this is Nimrod, because of whose evil thought the world uses not one language only. Let us leave him, and let us not speak in vain, for so is every language to him, as his to others, which to no one is known."

Then turning to the left, we pursued our way, and at a crossbow's shot we found the next, far more fierce and larger. Who the master was for binding him I cannot tell; but he had his right arm fastened behind, and the other in front, by a chain that held him entwined from the neck downward, so that upon his uncovered part it was wound as far as the fifth coil. "This proud one wished to make trial of his power against the supreme Jove," said my Leader, "wherefore he has such reward; Ephialtes [1] is his name, and he made his great en-

---

[1] Iphimedeia bore to Poseidon two sons, "but they were short-lived, godlike Otus and far-famed Ephialtes whom the fruitful

deavors when the giants made the Gods afraid;
the arms which he plied he moves nevermore."

And I to him, " If it may be, I should like my
eyes to have experience of the huge Briareus." [1]
Whereon he answered, " Thou shalt see Antaeus
close at hand here, who speaks, and is unbound,[2]
and will set us at the bottom of all sin.   Him
whom thou wishest to see is much farther on, and
is bound and fashioned like this one, save that he
seems more ferocious in his look."

Never was earthquake so mighty that it shook a
tower as violently as Ephialtes was quick to shake
himself.   Then more than ever did I fear death;
and there had been no need of more than the fright,
if I had not seen his bonds.

We then proceeded further forward, and came
to Antaeus, who full five ells, besides his head,
issued forth from the cavern.   " O thou that, in

Earth nourished to be the tallest and much the most beautiful of
mortals except renowned Orion, for at nine years old they were
nine cubits in breadth, and nine fathoms tall.   They even threat-
ened the immortals, raising the din of tumultuous war on Olympus, and strove to set Ossa upon Olympus and wood-clad Pelion
upon Ossa, in order to scale heaven.   But Jove destroyed them
both."   *Odyssey*, xi. 306–317.

   [1] " Him of the hundred hands whom the Gods call Briareus."
Iliad, i. 402.

   [2] Because he took no part in the war of his brethren against
the Gods.   What Dante tells of him is derived from Lucan,
Pharsalia, iv. 597 sqq.

the fateful valley which made Scipio the heir of glory when Hannibal and his followers turned their backs, didst bring of old a thousand lions for booty, — and it still seems credible that hadst thou been at the high war of thy brothers, the sons of the Earth would have conquered, — set us below, and disdain thou not to do so, where the cold locks up Cocytus. Make us not go to Tityus, nor to Typhon;[1] this one can give of that which here is longed for;[2] therefore stoop, and curl not thy snout. He yet can restore fame to thee in the world; for he is living, and still expects long life, if Grace doth not untimely call him to itself." Thus said the Master; and he in haste stretched out those hands, whose strong grip Hercules once felt, and took my Leader. Virgil, when he felt himself taken up, said to me, " Come hither so that I take thee." Then he made one bundle of himself and me. As beneath its leaning side, the Carisenda[3] seems to look when a cloud is going

---

[1] Lucan (*Phars.* iv. 600), naming these giants, says they were less strong than Antaeus; wherefore there is subtle flattery in these words of Virgil.

[2] To be remembered on earth.

[3] The more inclined of the two famous leaning towers at Bologna. As the cloud goes over it, the tower seems to bend to meet it. So Coleridge in his *Ode to Dejection:*

> And those thin clouds above, in flakes and bars,
> That give away their motion to the stars.

over so that the tower hangs counter to it, thus seemed Antaeus to me that stood attent to see him bend; and it was a moment when I could have wished to go by another road.   But lightly on the bottom that swallows Lucifer with Judas he set us down; nor, thus bent, did he there make stay, and like a mast in a ship he raised himself.

CANTO XXXII.

Ninth Circle : traitors. First ring : Caina. — Counts of
Mangona. — Camicion de' Pazzi. — Second ring : Antenoia.
— Bocca degli Abati. — Buoso da Duera. — Count Ugolino.

If I had rhymes both harsh and raucous, such
as would befit the dismal hole on which thrust [1]
all the other rocks, I would press out the juice of
my conception more fully; but since I have them
not, not without fear I bring myself to speak; for
to describe the bottom of the whole universe is no
enterprise to take up in jest, nor for a tongue that
cries *mamma* or *babbo*.   But may those Dames aid
my verse who aided Amphion to close in Thebes;
so that from the fact the speech be not diverse.

O populace miscreant above all, that art in the
place whereof to speak is hard, better had ye been
here [2] or sheep or goats !

When we were down in the dark abyss beneath
the feet of the giant, but far lower, and I was
gazing still at the high wall, I heard say to me,
" Beware how thou steppest ; take heed thou tram-

---

[1] Rest their weight.   [2] On earth.

ple not with thy soles the heads of the wretched weary brethren." Whereat I turned, and saw before me, and under my feet, a lake which through frost had semblance of glass and not of water.

The Danube in Austria makes not for its current so thick a veil in winter, nor the Don yonder under the cold sky, as there was here; for if Tambernich[1] had fallen thereupon, or Pietrapana,[2] it would not even at the edge have given a creak. And as to croak the frog lies with muzzle out of the water, what time[3] oft dreams the peasant girl of gleaning, so, livid up to where shame appears,[4] were the woeful shades within the ice, setting their teeth to the note of the stork.[5] Every one held his face turned downward; from the mouth the cold, and from the eyes the sad heart compels witness of itself among them.

When I had looked round awhile, I turned to my feet, and saw two so close that they had the hair of their heads mixed together. "Tell me, ye who so press tight your breasts," said I, "who are ye?" And they bent their necks, and after they had raised their faces to me, their eyes, which before were moist only within, gushed up through the

---

[1] A mountain, the locality of which is unknown.
[2] One of the Tuscan Apennines.
[3] In summer.
[4] Up to the face.
[5] Chattering with cold.

lids, and the frost bound the tears between them, and locked them up again. Clamp never girt board to board so strongly; wherefore they like two he-goats butted together, such anger overcame them.

And one who had lost both his ears through the cold, still with his face downward, said to me, " Why dost thou so mirror thyself on us? If thou wouldst know who are these two, the valley whence the Bisenzio descends belonged to their father Albert, and to them.[1] From one body they issued, and all Caina [2] thou mayst search, and thou wilt not find shade more worthy to be fixed in ice; not he whose breast and shadow were broken by one and the same blow by the hand of Arthur; [3] not Focaccia; [4] not he who encumbers me with his head, so that I cannot see beyond, and was named Sassol Mascheroni: [5] if thou art Tuscan, well knowest thou now who he was. And that thou mayst not put me to more speech, know that I was Camicion de' Pazzi,[6] and I await Carlino that ле may exonerate me."

[1] They were of the Alberti, counts of Mangona, in Tuscany, and had killed each other.

[2] The first division of this ninth and lowest circle of Hell.

[3] Mordred, the traitorous son of Arthur.

[4] From the crimes of Focaccia, a member of the great Cancellieri family of Pistoia, began the feud of the Black and the White factions, which long raged in Pistoia and in Florence.

[5] A Florentine who murdered his nephew for an inheritance.

[6] A murderer of one of his kinsmen, whose crime was surpassed

Then I saw a thousand faces made currish by the cold, whence shuddering comes to me, and will always come, at frozen pools.

And while we were going toward the centre [1] to which tends every weight, and I was trembling in the eternal shade, whether it was will, or destiny, or fortune I know not, but, walking among the heads, I struck my foot hard in the face of one. Wailing he cried out to me, " Why dost thou trample me? If thou comest not to increase the vengeance of Mont' Aperti, why dost thou molest me?" And I, " My Master, now wait here for me, so that I may free me from a doubt by means of this one, then thou shalt make me hasten as much as thou wilt." The Leader stopped, and I said to that shade who was bitterly blaspheming still, " Who art thou that thus railest at another?" " Now thou, who art thou, that goest through the Antenora," [2] he answered, " smiting the cheeks of others, so that if thou wert alive, it would be too much?" " Alive I am, and it may be dear to thee," was my reply, " if thou demandest fame,

by that of Carlino de' Pazzi, who, in 1302, betrayed a band of the Florentine exiles who had taken refuge in a stronghold of his in Valdarno.

[1] The centre of the earth.

[2] The second division of the ninth circle; so named after the Trojan who, though of good repute in Homer, was charged by a later tradition with having betrayed Troy.

that I should set thy name amid the other notes."
And he to me, "For the contrary do I long ; take
thyself hence, and give me no more trouble, for
ill thou knowest to flatter on this plain." Then
I took him by the hair of the crown, and said,
" It shall needs be that thou name thyself, or that
not a hair remain upon thee here." Whereon he
to me, " Though thou strip me of hair, I will not
tell thee who I am, nor will I show it to thee if a
thousand times thou fallest on my head."

I already had his hair twisted in my hand, and
had pulled out more than one shock, he barking,
with his eyes kept close down, when another cried
out, " What ails thee, Bocca?[1] Is it not enough
for thee to make music with thy jaws, but thou
must bark? What devil has hold of thee?"
" Now," said I, "I would not have thee speak,
accursed traitor, for to thy shame will I carry true
news of thee." "Begone," he answered, " and
relate what thou wilt, but be not silent, if from
here within thou goest forth, of him who now had
his tongue so ready. He weeps here the money of
the French ; I saw, thou canst say, him of Duera,[2]

---

[1] Bocca degli Abati, the most noted of Florentine traitors, who
in the heat of the battle of Mont' Aperti, in 1260, cut off the hand
of the standard-bearer of the cavalry, so that the standard fell,
and the Guelphs of Florence, disheartened thereby, were put to
rout with frightful slaughter.

[2] Buoso da Duera of Cremona, who, for a bribe, let pass near

there where the sinners stand cooling. Shouldst thou be asked who else was there, thou hast at thy side that Beccheria [1] whose gorget Florence cut. Gianni del Soldanier [2] I think is farther on with Ganellon [3] and Tribaldello,[4] who opened Faenza when it was sleeping."

We had now parted from him when I saw two frozen in one hole, so that the head of one was a hood for the other. And as bread is devoured in hunger, so the uppermost one set his teeth upon the other where the brain joins with the nape. Not otherwise Tydeus gnawed for spite the temples of Menalippus than this one did the skull and the other parts. " O thou! that by so bestial a sign showest hatred against him whom thou dost eat, tell me the wherefore," said I, " with this compact, that if thou rightfully of him complainest, I, knowing who ye are, and his sin, may yet recompense thee for it in the world above, if that with which I speak be not dried up."

Parma, without resistance, the cavalry of Charles of Anjou, led by Gui de Montfort to the conquest of Naples in 1265.

[1] Tesauro de' Beccheria, Abbot of Vallombrosa, and Papal Legate, beheaded by the Florentines in 1258, because of his treacherous dealings with the exiled Ghibellines.

[2] A Ghibelline leader, who, after the defeat of Manfred in 1266, plotted against his own party.

[3] Ganellon, the traitor who brought about the defeat at Roncesvalles.

[4] He betrayed Faenza to the French, in 1282.

CANTO XXXIII.

Ninth circle : traitors. Second ring : Antenora. — Count Ugolino. — Third ring : Ptolomæa. — Brother Alberigo. Branca d' Oria.

FROM his savage repast that sinner raised his mouth, wiping it with the hair of the head that he had spoiled behind : then he began, "Thou willest that I renew a desperate grief that oppresses my heart already only in thinking ere I speak of it. But, if my words are to be seed that may bear fruit of infamy for the traitor whom I gnaw, thou shalt see me speak and weep at once. I know not who thou art, nor by what mode thou art come down hither, but Florentine thou seemest to me truly when I hear thee. Thou hast to know that I was the Count Ugolino and he the Archbishop Ruggieri.[1] Now will I tell thee why I am such a

[1] In July, 1288, Ugolino della Gherardesca, Count of Donoratico, head of a faction of the Guelphs in Pisa, in order to deprive Nino of Gallura, head of the opposing faction, of the lordship of the city, treacherously joined forces with the Archbishop Ruggieri degli Ubaldini, head of the Ghibellines, and drove Nino and his followers from the city. The archbishop thereupon took advantage of the weakening of the Guelphs and excited the populace against Ugolino, charging him with having for a bribe restored

neighbor. That by the effect of his evil thoughts, I, trusting to him, was taken and then put to death, there is no need to tell. But that which thou canst not have heard, namely, how cruel was my death, thou shalt hear, and shalt know if he hath wronged me.

"A narrow slit in the mew, which from me has the name of Famine, and in which others yet must be shut up, had already shown me through its opening many moons, when I had the bad dream that rent for me the veil of the future.

"This one appeared to me master and lord, chasing the wolf and his whelps upon the mountain[1] for which the Pisans cannot see Lucca. With lean, eager, and trained hounds, Gualandi with Sismondi and with Lanfranchi[2] he had put before him at the front. After short course, the father and his sons seemed to me weary, and it seemed to me I saw their flanks torn by the sharp fangs.

to Florence and Lucca some of their towns of which the Pisans had made themselves masters. He, with his followers, attacked Count Ugolino in his house, took him prisoner, with two of his sons and two of his grandsons, and shut them up in the Tower of the Gualandi, where in the following March, on the arrival of Count Guido da Montefeltro (see Canto xxvii), as Captain of Pisa, they were starved to death.

[1] Monte San Giuliano.

[2] Three powerful Ghibelline families of Pisa.

" When I awoke before the morrow, I heard my sons, who were with me, wailing in their sleep, and asking for bread. Truly thou art cruel if already thou grievest not, thinking on what my heart foretold ; and if thou weepest not, at what art thou wont to weep ? Now they were awake, and the hour drew near when food was wont to be brought to us, and because of his dream each one was apprehensive. And I heard the door below of the horrible tower locking up; whereat I looked on the faces of my sons without saying a word. I wept not, I was so turned to stone within. They wept ; and my poor little Anselm said, ' Thou lookest so, father, what aileth thee ? ' Yet I did not weep ; nor did I answer all that day, nor the night after, until the next sun came out upon the world. When a little ray entered the woeful prison, and I discerned by their four faces my own very aspect, both my hands I bit for woe ; and they, thinking I did it through desire of eating, of a sudden rose, and said, ' Father, it will be far less pain to us if thou eat of us ; thou didst clothe us with this wretched flesh, and do thou strip it off.' I quieted me then, not to make them more sad : that day and the next we all stayed dumb. Ah, thou hard earth ! why didst thou not open ? After we had come to the fourth day, Gaddo threw himself stretched out at my feet, saying,

'My father, why dost thou not help me?' Here he died: and, even as thou seest me, I saw the three fall one by one between the fifth day and the sixth; then I betook me, already blind, to groping over each, and two days I called them after they were dead: then fasting had more power than grief."

When he had said this, with his eyes distorted, he seized again the wretched skull with his teeth, that were strong as a dog's upon the bone.

Ah Pisa! reproach of the people of the fair country where the *sì* doth sound,[1] since thy neighbors are slow to punish thee, let Caprara and Gorgona[2] move and make a hedge for Arno at its mouth, so that it drown every person in thee; for if Count Ugolino had repute of having betrayed thee in thy towns, thou oughtest not to have set his sons on such a cross. Their young age, thou modern Thebes! made Uguccione and the Brigata innocent, and the other two that the song names above.

We passed onward to where the ice roughly enswathes another folk, not turned downward, but all upon their backs. Their very weeping lets

---

[1] Italy, whose language Dante calls *il volgare di sì.* (*Convito,* i. 10.)

[2] Two little islands not far from the mouth of the Arno, on whose banks Pisa lies.

them not weep, and the pain that finds a barrier on the eyes turns inward to increase the anguish; for the first tears form a block, and like a visor of crystal fill all the cup beneath the eyebrow.

And although, because of the cold, as from a callus, all feeling had left its abode in my face, it now seemed to me I felt some wind, wherefore I, "My Master, who moves this? Is not every vapor [1] quenched here below?" Whereon he to me, "Speedily shalt thou be where thine eye shall make answer to thee of this, beholding the cause that rains down the blast."

And one of the wretches of the cold crust cried out to us, "O souls so cruel that the last station is given to you, lift from my eyes the hard veils, so that I may vent the grief that swells my heart, a little ere the weeping re-congeal!" Wherefore I to him, "If thou wilt that I relieve thee, tell me who thou art, and if I rid thee not, may it be mine to go to the bottom of the ice." He replied then, "I am friar Alberigo; [2] I am he of the

---

[1] Wind being supposed to be caused by the action of the sun on the vapors of the atmosphere.

[2] Alberigo de' Manfredi, of Faenza; one of the Jovial Friars (see Canto xxiii). Having received a blow from one of his kinsmen, he pretended to forgive it, and invited him and his son to a feast. Toward the end of the meal he gave a preconcerted signal by calling out, "Bring the fruit," upon which his emissaries rushed in and killed the two guests. The "fruit of Brother Alberigo" became a proverb.

fruits of the bad garden, and here I receive a date
for a fig."[1] "Oh!" said I to him; "art thou now
already dead?" And he to me, "How it may go
with my body in the world above I bear no knowledge. Such vantage hath this Ptolomæa[2] that
oftentime the soul falls hither ere Atropos hath
given motion to it.[3] And that thou may the more
willingly scrape the glassy tears from my face,
know that soon as the soul betrays, as I did, its
body is taken from it by a demon, who thereafter
governs it until its time be all revolved. The soul
falls headlong into this cistern, and perchance the
body of the shade that here behind me winters still
appears above; thou oughtest to know him if thou
comest down but now. He is Ser Branca d' Oria,[4]
and many years have passed since he was thus shut
up." "I think," said I to him, " that thou deceiv-
est me, for Branca d' Oria is not yet dead, and he
eats, and drinks, and sleeps, and puts on clothes."
"In the ditch of the Malebranche above," he said,
"there where the tenacious pitch is boiling, Michel
Zanche[5] had not yet arrived when this one left

[1] A fig is the cheapest of Tuscan fruits; the imported date is
more costly.

[2] The third ring of ice, named for that Ptolemy of Jericho who
slew his father-in-law, the high-priest Simon, and his sons
(1 Maccabees xvi. 11–16).

[3] That is, before its life on earth is ended.

[4] Murderer, in 1275, of his father-in-law, Michel Zanche.

[5] Already heard of in the fifth pit (Canto xxii. 88).

in his own stead a devil in his body, and in that of one of his near kin, who committed the treachery together with him. But now stretch out hither thy hand; open my eyes for me." And I opened them not for him, and to be rude to him was courtesy.

Ah Genoese! men strange to all morality and full of all corruption, why are ye not scattered from the world? For with the worst spirit of Romagna I found one of you such that for his deeds in soul he is bathed in Cocytus, and in body he seems still alive on earth.

CANTO XXXIV.

Ninth Circle : traitors. Fourth ring : Judecca. — Luci=
fer. — Judas, Brutus and Cassius. — Centre of the universe.
— Passage from Hell. — Ascent to the surface of the South=
ern Hemisphere.

" *Vexilla regis prodeunt inferni*,[1] toward us ;
therefore look in front," said my Master ; " if thou
discernest him." As a mill that the wind turns
seems from afar when a thick fog breathes, or
when our hemisphere grows dark with night, such
a structure then it seemed to me I saw.

Then, because of the wind, I drew me behind
my Leader ; for there was no other shelter. I
was now, and with fear I put it in verse, there[2]
where the shades were wholly covered, and showed
through like a straw in glass. Some are lying ;
some stand erect, this on his head, and that on his
soles ; another like a bow inverts his face to his
feet.

[1] "The banners of the King of Hell advance." *Vexilla Regis
prodeunt* are the first words of a hymn in honor of the Cross,
sung at vespers on the Feast of the Exaltation of the Holy Cross
and on Monday of Holy Week.

[2] In the fourth, innermost ring of ice of the ninth circle, — the
Judecca.

When we had gone so far forward that it pleased
my Master to show me the creature that had the
fair semblance, from before me he took himself
and made me stop, saying, "Behold Dis, and behold the place where it is needful that with forti-
tude thou arm thee." How I became then chilled
and hoarse, ask it not, Reader, for I write it not,
because all speech would be little. I did not die,
and I did not remain alive. Think now for thyself,
if thou hast grain of wit, what I became, deprived
of one and the other.

The emperor of the woeful realm from his mid-
breast issued forth from the ice; and I match
better with a giant, than the giants do with his
arms. See now how great must be that whole
which corresponds to such parts. If he was as
fair as he now is foul, and against his Maker lifted
up his brow, surely may all tribulation proceed
from him. Oh how great a marvel it seemed to
me, when I saw three faces on his head! one in
front, and that was red; the others were two
that were joined to this above the very middle of
each shoulder, and they were joined together at
the place of the crest; and the right seemed between white and yellow, the left was such to sight
as those who come from where the Nile flows
valleyward. Beneath each came forth two great
wings, of size befitting so huge a bird. Sails of

the sea never saw I such. They had no feathers, but their fashion was of a bat; and he was flapping them so that three winds went forth from him, whereby Cocytus was all congealed. With six eyes he was weeping, and over three chins trickled the tears and bloody drivel. With each mouth he was crushing a sinner with his teeth, in manner of a brake, so that he thus was making three of them woeful. To the one in front the biting was nothing to the clawing, so that sometimes his spine remained all stripped of skin.

"That soul up there which has the greatest punishment," said the Master, "is Judas Iscariot, who has his head within, and plies his legs outside. Of the other two who have their heads down, he who hangs from the black muzzle is Brutus; see how he writhes and says no word; and the other is Cassius, who seems so large-limbed. But the night is rising again, and now we must depart, for we have seen the whole."

As was his pleasure, I clasped his neck, and he took opportunity of time and place, and when the wings were opened wide he caught hold on the shaggy flanks; from shag to shag he then descended between the bushy hair and the frozen crusts. When we were just where the thigh turns on the thick of the haunch, my Leader, with effort and stress of breath, turned his head where he had his shanks, and clambered by the hair as a man that ascends, so that I thought to return again to hell.

"Cling fast hold," said the Master, panting like one weary, "for by such stairs it behoves to depart from so much evil." Then he came forth through the opening of a rock, and placed me upon its edge to sit; then stretched toward me his cautious step.

I raised my eyes, and thought to see Lucifer as I had left him, and I saw him holding his legs upward. And if I then became perplexed, let the dull folk think it that see not what that point is that I had passed.[1]

"Rise up," said the Master, "on thy feet; the way is long and the road is difficult, and already the sun unto mid-tierce [2] returns."

---

[1] This point is the centre of the universe; when Virgil had turned upon the haunch of Lucifer, the passage had been made from one hemisphere of the earth — the inhabited and known hemisphere — to the other where no living men dwell, and where the only land is the mountain of Purgatory. In changing one hemisphere for the other there is a change of time of twelve hours. A second Saturday morning begins for the poets, and they pass nearly as long a time as they have been in Hell, that is, twenty-four hours, in traversing the long and hard way that leads through the new hemisphere on which they have just entered.

[2] Tierce is the church office sung at the third hour of the day, and the name is given to the first three hours after sunrise. Mid-tierce consequently here means about half-past seven o'clock. In

It was no hallway of a palace where we were,
but a natural dungeon that had a bad floor, and
lack of light. " Before I tear me from the abyss,"
said I when I had risen up, " my Master, speak a
little to me to draw me out of error. Where is the
ice? and this one, how is he fixed thus upside
down? and how in such short while has the sun
from eve to morn made transit?" And he to me,
"Thou imaginest that thou still art on the other side
of the centre where I laid hold on the hair of the
guilty Worm that pierces the world. On that side
wast thou so long as I descended; when I turned
thou didst pass the point to which from all parts
whatever has weight is drawn; and thou art now
arrived beneath the hemisphere opposite to that
which the great dry land covers, and beneath whose
zenith the Man was slain who was born and lived
without sin. Thou hast thy feet upon the little
sphere which forms the other face of the Judecca.
Here it is morning when there it is evening; and
he who made for us a stairway with his hair is still
fixed even as he was before. Upon this side he
fell down from heaven, and the earth, which before
was spread out here, through fear of him made of
the sea a veil, and came to your hemisphere; and

Hell Dante never mentions the sun to mark division of time, but
now, having issued from Hell, Virgil marks the hour by a reference to the sun.

CPSIA information can be obtained
at www.ICGtesting.com
Printed in the USA
LVHW010908050119
602872LV00021B/977/P